TEACHING EARLy yEARS

PRAISE FOR THE BOOK

Teaching Early Years takes key aspects of theory and effectively explains and exemplifies them through the lens of the practitioner. The case studies in each chapter enable trainees to discuss and reflect on their theoretical knowledge in real-life contexts and support their professional development. The book brings together the different UK early years curricula so that trainees also gain an understanding of the varying approaches and age ranges that they cover. Thomas and McInnes have produced a most useful and practical text that will enable early years teachers to support the holistic development of young children in their care.

Sally Pearse, Head of Area 0-5 Teacher Training, Sheffield Institute of Education

Throughout this book, practitioners have worked alongside academics to provide the reader with a fresh perspective on the early years curriculum, particularly on play and playfulness, setting theory into meaningful contexts for practitioners. The text celebrates the uniqueness of the early years and helps readers to reflect on their own personal pedagogies around play and develop clear professional identities about what it means to teach young children.

The book is an engaging and accessible read, which would be particularly useful for students of early childhood education and for students training to be early years teachers. The practical examples also make this essential reading for current practitioners in early years and the early primary phase.

Patricia Burgess, Programme Lead for Early Years Teacher Status, Edge Hill University

Teaching Early Years provides a fresh take on the effective translation of an early years curriculum into practice. It advocates an early years pedagogy, which is experiential in nature and playful in approach, but also explicitly emphasises the role of the early years practitioner in the learning process. Teaching Early Years will be an invaluable resource for any student studying early childhood studies or training to teach at early years or primary levels. This book is also ideal for early years and primary practitioners. Although focused principally on a Welsh and English context, this book has much to offer Early Years students and practitioners across the globe.

Glenda Walsh, Head of Early Years Education, Stranmillis University College

The strength of this very accessible book is the breadth of the practice and academic backgrounds of the contributors as well as the range of relevant areas covered. It is particularly helpful to have a specific focus on well-being in the early years and the vital importance of understanding child development, alongside maths, science and English.

Eunice Lumsden, Head of Early Years, University of Northampton

TEACHING EARLY YEARS
theory and practice

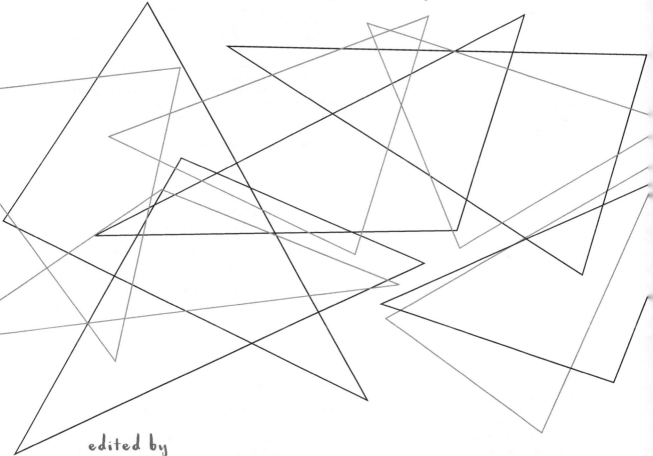

edited by
AMANDA THOMAS AND KAREN MCINNES

SAGE

Los Angeles | London | New Delhi
Singapore | Washington DC | Melbourne

Los Angeles | London | New Delhi
Singapore | Washington DC | Melbourne

SAGE Publications Ltd
1 Oliver's Yard
55 City Road
London EC1Y 1SP

SAGE Publications Inc.
2455 Teller Road
Thousand Oaks, California 91320

SAGE Publications India Pvt Ltd
B 1/I 1 Mohan Cooperative Industrial Area
Mathura Road
New Delhi 110 044

SAGE Publications Asia-Pacific Pte Ltd
3 Church Street
#10-04 Samsung Hub
Singapore 049483

Editorial Arrangement © Amanda Thomas and Karen McInnes, 2018

Chapter 1 © Amanda Thomas and Karen McInnes, 2018
Chapter 2 © Claire Pescott, 2018
Chapter 3 © Karen McInnes and Holly Gallan, 2018
Chapter 4 © Karen McInnes and Natacha Yuen, 2018
Chapter 5 © Alyson Lewis and Lucy Rees, 2018
Chapter 6 © Rhiannon Packer, Philippa Watkins and Marc Hughes, 2018
Chapter 7 © Catherine Jones, 2018
Chapter 8 © Amanda Thomas, Karen Parker, Carole Carter and Clare Griffiths, 2018
Chapter 9 © Catherine Jones and Francine Davies, 2018
Chapter 10 © Alyson Lewis and Rebecca Poole, 2018
Chapter 11 © Amanda Thomas and Karen McInnes, 2018

First published 2018

Editor: Jude Bowen
Editorial assistant: Catriona McMullen
Associate editor: George Knowles
Production editor: Tom Bedford
Copyeditor: Elaine Leek
Proofreader: Aud Scriven
Indexer: Silvia Benvenuto
Marketing manager: Lorna Patkai
Cover design: Wendy Scott
Typeset by: C&M Digitals (P) Ltd, Chennai, India
Printed in the UK

Library of Congress Control Number: 2017935517

British Library Cataloguing in Publication data

A catalogue record for this book is available from the British Library

ISBN 978-1-4739-4625-5
ISBN 978-1-4739-4626-2 (pbk)

At SAGE we take sustainability seriously. Most of our products are printed in the UK using FSC papers and boards. When we print overseas we ensure sustainable papers are used as measured by the PREPS grading system. We undertake an annual audit to monitor our sustainability.

CONTENTS

LIST OF TABLES

LIST OF FIGURES

ABOUT THE EDITORS AND CONTRIBUTORS

Editors

Amanda Thomas is currently a Senior Lecturer in Early Years Education at the University of South Wales, delivering on a range of education modules. In 1997, she began teaching in a primary school and successfully led the Early Years provision. Amanda also taught in FE for four years, training childcare practitioners. She is currently researching schemas in the Foundation Phase for her PhD.

Karen McInnes has recently moved to Norland College as Research Fellow. Previously she was Programme Leader: Postgraduate and International, in the Institute for Education at Bath Spa University. She has been an Award Leader for the MSc Play Therapy and MSc Play and Therapeutic Play at the University of South Wales, and completed her PhD in play and learning in the early years and qualified as a play therapist whilst there. She has also been a Senior Researcher with Barnardo's UK Policy and Research Team, researching various issues affecting children and their families and making policy recommendations based on her research. Karen has extensive experience working with young children as a play therapist, speech therapist and teacher. She has published on various aspects of early years education and play and is the co-author of *The Essence of Play* (Routledge, 2013).

Contributors

Carole Carter has been a Nursery Teacher in a primary school for the past sixteen years. She trained initially as a nursery nurse and then achieved HLTA status, a teaching qualification and an assessor's award in childcare. She also teaches Art and RE for PPA cover throughout Key Stages 1 and 2.

Francine Davies is a freelance artist, working creatively with children and adults. With a degree in Geography and Geology, she focuses on perspective as a physical and emotional quality influencing people and places. With qualifications in counselling, youth and community work she has developed support and educational services for children.

Holly Gallan is currently training to become a primary school teacher through the University of Gloucestershire. She obtained an MSc in Play and Therapeutic Play at the University of South Wales, where she was awarded outstanding student for her research comparing educators', parents' and children's perceptions of play, and she has a BSc in Psychology. Holly has experience of working with children and other educators in her role as a Teaching Assistant and as an Emotional Literacy Support Assistant.

Clare Griffiths achieved a degree in Child Psychology at the University of Glamorgan. Following this, she has worked for the past nine years as a practitioner in Early Years. Clare is also the Special Needs Coordinator and her specialism is English.

Marc Hughes is currently an acting Deputy Headteacher of a three-form-entry primary school in Wales. He has previously taught in many different settings, including being the headteacher of a two-form-entry primary school in a recognised deprived area of South Wales where 56% of the pupils were entitled to free school meals. Before that, he worked for a number of years in a primary school where over 90% of pupils considered English as an Additional Language. He has also taught in three other schools with very different settings in South Wales.

Catherine Jones is an Academic Manager focusing on Innovation and Technology in Learning and Teaching at the University of South Wales. Originally a primary and special needs teacher, her teaching focuses on policy into practice and technology-enhanced learning. Her research interests include collaborative learning, technology-enhanced learning, evaluating professional practice and innovative pedagogies.

Alyson Lewis is a Senior Lecturer in Early Years Education at Bath Spa University. She has ten years' experience of working as an Early Years teacher. Her PhD explores how well-being is understood and operationalised in the Early Years curriculum. She also co-authored *An Introduction to the Foundation Phase in Wales* (2016).

Rhiannon Packer is a Senior Lecturer at the University of South Wales and delivers on the Words Matters, Numbers Count module as well as Inclusive Practice in the Early Years. She is a Fellow of the Higher Education Academy and Associate Member of the British Dyslexia Association. She worked for nine years as a Welsh teacher and has written a number of books for Welsh learners in Key Stages 2 and 3.

Karen Parker is the Manager at the University of South Wales Child Care Services Department. She has a first-class honours BSc Childhood Studies Degree, a QCF Level 5 Management in Childcare and Education, and a Level 3 Forest Leader qualification. She has led the team to achieve very positive CSSIW and Estyn inspection results and a Healthy and Sustainable Pre-school setting status. She worked previously in a range of private day care facilities as a nursery nurse since 1981.

Claire Pescott is a Senior Lecturer in Early Years and Education at the University of South Wales. Prior to this appointment, she was a primary level teacher for eleven years and taught all ages and children with special needs. Her research interests include social media and authenticity, and creative participatory research methods.

Rebecca Poole has thirteen years' experience of working as an Early Years Teaching Assistant in primary schools. She has a first-class honours degree in Early Education from Bath Spa University and is currently completing her PGCE. Her research projects have focused on the value of outdoor play for language and physical development.

Lucy Rees is an Early Years Foundation Stage teacher. She has been teaching for twenty years, specialising in Early Years education. She believes passionately in quality early years experiences provided through a child-centred approach to learning.

Philippa Watkins is currently a Lecturer at the University of South Wales and a fellow of the Higher Education Academy. She worked for twelve years as an English teacher, and was Head of English for four years before moving to the higher education sector, where she has worked for eight years. She delivers on the Words Matter, Numbers Count module on the BA Early Year, Education and Practice module.

Natacha Yuen qualified as a primary school teacher in 1990 and has worked in a number of different primary schools across the UK, including becoming the leader of a small Early Years setting. She developed her practice by achieving Early Years Professional Status, becoming a lead teacher within various different children's centres across Bristol. She is currently a Deputy Head and Lead Teacher at Hartcliffe Nursery School and Children's Centre and delivers CPD across South Bristol.

ACKNOWLEDGEMENTS

The authors would like to thank all the children, parents and practitioners who let us into their settings, classrooms and lives to observe and talk about their experiences. We have all learnt a lot in the process and hope we have conveyed this learning in the different chapters to show how theory links with practice. We would also like to thank our colleague Jacqui Harrett who inspired the book.

INTRODUCTION

Amanda Thomas and Karen McInnes

This book arose from a need to have a text that integrates both theory and practice across the Early Years and early primary phase. It is intended to fill a gap in the current market for students studying education in the Early Years and early primary phase. Many of the books available for students concentrate on theory without necessarily setting this theory in meaningful contexts. This book aims to integrate both the 'why' and the 'how' by giving a theoretical background to areas of the curriculum combined with sections on how that theory looks in practice. Each chapter will examine an area of learning from the theoretical perspective followed by examples of work in practice which are likely to be a mix of case studies, lesson plans, examples of comments from teachers and work by children. This innovative approach should enable students to make sense of the theories that form the foundation for teaching and learning in a manner they are able to relate to. By seeing theory in practice, students may be able to make more sense of important aspects of both teaching and learning, so enhancing their knowledge of how young children think and learn.

It is the intention of the authors that it should be an edited book with chapters covering the Early Years areas of learning in the first instance and with scope for developing those areas further into the primary phase. Contributors are a mix of both academics and teachers, giving a balanced and creative approach to the topic. This unique mix of authorship will enable the connections between theory and practice to be explicitly linked and embed the theory in current educational practice.

Play and playfulness in the curriculum will be an overarching theme throughout the book. Current research highlighting the importance of the voice of the child in enabling adults to understand play and playfulness will be presented. It will be demonstrated that this approach facilitates motivation, confidence and involvement in learning and is applicable across the Early Years and primary phases. Playfulness, being creative and 'thinking outside the box' usually result in more motivated children or pupils. This may also be applied to those teaching children and this book aims to provide students with examples of activities to help them to develop their own creativity.

Key features of the book are:

- An innovative approach to bridging the theory/practice divide
- A fresh perspective on delivering the curriculum
- A varied selection of authors from both academia and schools

Pedagogical features

As this book is a demonstration of theory in practice it will have a mixture of features, including case studies of children, short summaries of chapters, lesson plans, classroom activities and suggestions for reading in the concluding chapter. It will have a mixture of seminal research and topical research conducted during the writing of the book to ensure that it is topical as well as based on solid foundations of knowledge.

A unique feature of this book is the connection between theory and practice, with case studies highlighting how theory translates into pedagogy and these will be examined in detail. Case studies have been taken from Early Years practice from 0 to 7 years and in English and Welsh settings. The rationale behind using examples from England and Wales is to highlight the differences in the Welsh Foundation Phase and English Early Years Foundation Stage (EYFS). The Foundation Phase spans the age range 3–7 years and the Early Years Foundation Stage covers 0–5 years and by using the two curricula this book highlights the similarities and differences between them. It also highlights how Early Years practitioners in English settings can extend a playful pedagogy beyond the age of 5 years. The book also considers links between home and school, observation and assessment, and transition within and between settings. Each chapter has questions for practitioners to reflect upon their own practice and further reading to extend knowledge and understanding.

Chapter 1: Introduction

Amanda Thomas, Senior Lecturer, University of South Wales and Karen McInnes, Programme Leader: Postgraduate and International, Bath Spa University

In this chapter the authors provide a rationale to the book. They offer an introduction to the themes included in the book with an overview of what to expect in each chapter and how to use this book.

Chapter 2: What can we learn from UK Early Years curricula?

Claire Pescott, Senior Lecturer, University of South Wales

This is more theoretical than the other chapters in this book and, unlike the others, is sole authored. However, the author is a new academic, having recently been an Early Years practitioner. An overview of curriculum frameworks currently operating in the UK will be critically analysed: the Early Years Foundation Stage in England, the Foundation Phase in Wales, the Curriculum for Excellence in Scotland and the Foundation Stage in Northern Ireland. Commonalities across the frameworks will be examined and then the Welsh Foundation Phase will be used as an exemplar of planning within an Early Years curriculum framework.

Chapter 3: Child development in practice

Karen McInnes, Programme Leader: Postgraduate and International, Bath Spa University and Holly Gallan, trainee primary school teacher and therapeutic play practitioner

This chapter will look at key areas of child development and identify how practitioners should use knowledge of child development in their practice. Drawing on case studies and interviews with practitioners, the authors will discuss what practitioners need to know about child development and how this knowledge will provide them with an evidence base from which to assess children's development and plan for their learning. It will also consider how this knowledge facilitates inter-agency working as well as enabling meaningful links between settings and home.

Chapter 4: Play and playfulness: The foundation of learning and development

Karen McInnes, Programme Leader: Postgraduate and International, Bath Spa University and Natacha Yuen, Deputy Headteacher at Hartcliffe Children's Centre, Bristol

This chapter explores the importance of play and playfulness for both the very young and for all children. An overview of how an Early Years curriculum is embedded in play will be provided along with its historical and theoretical underpinnings. Drawing on research evidence, a distinction will be made between play and playfulness and how children's views of play need to be listened to in order to truly provide a play-based curriculum. It will also be argued that playfulness provides the foundation of a positive relationship between practitioners and children to facilitate learning and development. Case studies will be used to show practitioners how they might ensure their provision and practice are more play-based and enable children to learn in a more playful way.

Chapter 5: Understanding well-being in the Early Years

Alyson Lewis, Senior Lecturer in Early Years Education at Bath Spa University and Lucy Rees, Early Years Foundation Stage teacher

Well-being is a complex, multi-dimensional concept and a term frequently used in policy and by practitioners, yet it is under-researched in education. This chapter explores the concept of well-being and what it means from different perspectives. It also discusses how well-being is enacted by practitioners in Early Years classrooms and provides useful ways of facilitating this. Well-being is often something that needs to be measured and the chapter discusses this complexity.

Chapter 6: Playing with words – becoming a reader and writer

Rhiannon Packer and Philippa Watkins, lecturers at the University of South Wales, and Marc Hughes, acting Deputy Headteacher of a Welsh primary school

Literacy development is essential as a foundation for all areas of the curriculum. This chapter examines the relationship between speaking, listening, reading and writing, and ways to engage young children in meaningful talk as a precursor for reading and writing. It embeds good practice in literacy by providing examples of how classroom practitioners employ a playful pedagogy to enthuse and engage learners in Early Years classrooms. The chapter discusses providing the right classroom environment for the development of effective communication skills and how children acquire language skills. It provides examples of case studies that reflect the need for children to be given opportunities to become readers and writers. In addition, the chapter provides opportunities to reflect upon providing learners with purpose and audiences for their writing to be meaningful.

Chapter 7: Developing mathematical confidence in the Early Years

Catherine Jones, Academic Manager of Innovation and Technology at the University of South Wales

Mathematical development has always been an important area of learning when planning a child's learning journey. The language of mathematics is so crucial and the integration of this across all other areas of learning ensures a child is exposed to concepts at an early age. Contexts for learning need to be developed with this in mind to ensure a child has a natural wonder and enthusiasm to build foundations for the future. This chapter discusses how mathematics needs to be taught in a meaningful way and how children develop their mathematical abilities. It is distinct from the other chapters as it focuses on how undergraduates view maths and how ICT can inform mathematical pedagogy, and is written solely by an academic.

The reader is provided with cases studies that explore the links between theory and practice and how mathematical development fits in with the rest of the Early Years and primary curriculum from an undergraduate point of view.

Chapter 8: Becoming a scientist through an experiential pedagogy

Amanda Thomas, Senior Lecturer, University of South Wales, Carole Carter and Clare Griffiths, classroom practitioners, and Karen Parker, Children Centre manager

To young children the world about them is a fascinating place and this chapter shows how to develop that natural curiosity through making and doing. From experimenting with things in the world about them children develop their natural curiosity and investigative skills as a basis for further learning. The chapter will focus on children in a Nursery and Reception class, and children aged 0–3 in a day care setting. There will be discussions on how children 'come to know' through hands-on learning and how this is translated into practice in the classroom. There will be case studies, discussions with classroom practitioners on their practice and observations of the children during science activities. There will be links made to the Early Years curriculum and discussions of different theories on how children construct knowledge and how current pedagogy supports this. Photographs of children's work (anonymous) will be included and there will be questions to consider that will allow the reader to reflect upon the issues raised.

Chapter 9: Inspiring creativity in the Early Years

Catherine Jones, Academic Manager of Innovation and Technology at the University of South Wales, and Francine Davies, freelance artist

Creativity is often regarded as the byproduct of art and music but this chapter shows how creative activities are reflected in every topic across the curriculum. From story-making and incorporating poetry and play we gain an insight into how creative children can be and how creativity in children is a valuable outlet for self-expression. This chapter is distinct in that it is written in a more subjective way, reflecting the personal nature of creativity and how it can be viewed differently by different people. Furthermore, it can provide the stepping stones that bridge the gap between the varying development of motor skills and cognitive skills among children. Readers will also be shown the importance of reflecting upon their own creativity in order to provide opportunities for children to be creative. There will be a discussion on how creativity fits into the current primary curriculum and how the theories behind the importance of creative development impact on practitioner practice. Evidence will be included from the workshops Francine runs in primary schools and her own experiences of how being creative helps children develop skills in other areas of learning. There will be questions included to allow the reader to reflect upon some of the issues raised in this chapter and how they can develop their own creative practice in the classroom.

Chapter 10: Into the great outdoors: Opportunities and experiences

Alyson Lewis, Senior Lecturer in Early Years Education at Bath Spa University, and Rebecca Poole, Early Years PGCE trainee teacher

A historical perspective of the outdoor classroom is provided which attempts to show the reader how traditional theorists have influenced 21st century thinking about the outdoors and risk-taking. Alyson Lewis demonstrates the benefits of learning outdoors and, in particular, discusses the importance of the Forest School approach, which is gaining momentum. This chapter also explores the role of the adult and highlights some of the challenges faced by practitioners in facilitating outdoor learning. The concept of 'risky play' is explored and its importance in child development. The chapter examines case studies that highlight the importance of using the outdoors and why, in Wales in particular, outdoor learning is an essential part of the Foundation Phase curriculum. The chapter reflects upon using the local outdoor environment for providing and extending learning opportunities for children.

Chapter 11: Conclusion

Amanda Thomas, Senior Lecturer, University of South Wales, and Karen McInnes, Programme Leader: Postgraduate and International, Bath Spa University

This book makes a key contribution by linking theory to practice and enabling the reader to contextualise the way children think and learn, and in this final chapter the editors summarise the learning resulting from the chapters and what can be gained from academics and practitioners working together. They will analyse and discuss common themes across the chapters which will be useful for supporting and extending Early Years practice. They will summarise how practitioners should continue their engagement with academic and theoretical learning in order to support the children they work with and so that, jointly, children and practitioners can become lifelong learners.

WHAT CAN WE LEARN FROM UK EARLY YEARS CURRICULA?

Claire Pescott

Reading this chapter will help you to understand the importance and relevance of utilising a curriculum framework and how this will impact on the quality of provision provided in Early Years settings. This chapter focuses on an overview of curriculum frameworks currently operating in the UK. Each of the four curricula will be presented: the Foundation Phase in Wales, the Early Years Foundation Stage in England, Curriculum for Excellence in Scotland and the Foundation Stage in Northern Ireland. Each curriculum will be explained briefly and a commonality between them considered. Utilising the Foundation Phase (Wales) as an example, an exploration of planning, the importance of learning through play and links to theory will demonstrate how learning, teaching and assessment are derived from frameworks and adapted to suit the needs of Early Years pupils. A case study will demonstrate the integral role of effective planning to support a child's developmental requirements. Using and interpreting a curriculum is crucial to the successful implementation of the teaching, learning and assessment processes within any country's educational system (Boyle and Charles, 2016). Understanding the implications of this and the intrinsic nature of the three components of learning, teaching and assessment is essential for all practitioners working within the Early Years.

In this chapter you will:

- Examine and explore UK curricula
- Look at the Foundation Phase as an example of UK curricula
- Explore international perspectives in relation to UK curricula
- Appreciate a curriculum as a framework for planning, observation and assessment

Key words

curricula, curriculum, pedagogy, framework, assessment, planning, holistic, experiential, teaching, learning, differentiation, play

Theoretical perspectives

Pedagogy versus curriculum

There is often some confusion between the terms 'pedagogy' and 'curriculum' and they are sometimes incorrectly used interchangeably. In simplistic terms, 'pedagogy' refers to the art or the science of teaching (Allen and Whalley, 2010), the mechanics or process that underpins it. It can also be viewed as a cohesive entity of theory and practice that draws on philosophy, psychology and social science (Cameron, 2006). It is fundamentally the process itself of learning and teaching and the systems that are in place to facilitate this. A curriculum is essentially a framework, a guide to be utilised and implemented in a practical way. Practitioners would agree that it is essential to follow and implement a curriculum when teaching the Early Years; this ensures the necessary breadth and coverage of different areas of learning, and it considers progression, differentiation and assessment with, ideally, a cohesive, holistic approach. Curriculum models for Early Years reflect varying beliefs and values that underpin the pedagogy, with play being the common denominator between each of the four UK curricula being examined. The juxtaposition of the approach is apparent with practitioners having an ethical and professional responsibility to interpret the framework and make subsequent informed decisions as well as the children's response to this, which is dependent on a multi-faceted dimension of diversity, e.g. gender, ethnicity, religion, culture, social class and additional or special needs (Wood, 2013).

Table 2.1 illustrates the policy frameworks in the UK (Wales, England, Northern Ireland and Scotland) and their stance on play and curriculum content.

UK curricula

As portrayed in Table 2.1, there are parallels between the UK curricula in terms of areas of learning, implementation of assessment and the overarching emphasis of play being central to Early Years learning and teaching. The age ranges for each curriculum are wide-ranging, with the EYFS (England) (DfE, 2014) commencing at birth and the Curriculum for Excellence (Scotland) being longitudinal in nature (up to 18 years). Although Wales has a separate curriculum for Early Years (3–7 years), this will be changing imminently; *A Curriculum for Wales – A Curriculum for Life* will be piloted from 2018 and will adopt a cross key stages approach from 3 to 16 years. Each curriculum has areas of learning rather than distinct and separate subjects, and whilst they have different titles, similarities occur with an emphasis on personal development, and literacy and numeracy. In Wales, a Welsh Development component is additional to reflect the bilingual culture.

The philosophy of play is a distinctive feature of all UK curricula and consequently demonstrates the importance of this approach to children's development. The four UK frameworks have their own version of what constitutes 'educational play' but it can be seen as an approach in school settings across the country. In Scotland play is integral to the Early Years curriculum and teachers are advised to create an environment that provides rich play opportunities to meet the needs of young children (Education Scotland, 2016). Similarly, for Northern Ireland, a stipulation is made to ensure that play is the adopted approach for academic and social development. The Foundation Stage in England also emphasises the importance of the play environment but also acknowledges that each child is unique and practitioners need to get to know each individual child (Palaiologou, 2016). Likewise, a play-based approach and active learning is advocated in Wales and is fundamental to the Foundation Phase (Wood, 2013). The importance of this notion being understood by all stakeholders is also validated as an essential component of this curriculum as well as a mix of adult-led and child-initiated play (WAG, 2008b). However, it is important to note that the rhetoric and reality of play is an issue across all UK curricula and more formalised and didactic approaches are becoming common practice.

Assessment is a key difference between the UK curricula: in England, children have the Early Years Foundation Stage Profile completed by the end of Reception (though this is under review at time of writing), a phonics

Table 2.1 UK curricula

	Wales	England	Northern Ireland	Scotland
Government department	Department for Children, Education , Lifelong Learning and Skills (DCELLS)	Department for Education (DfE)	Council for Curriculum, Examinations and Assessment (CCEA)	Education Scotland
Policy name	Foundation Phase	Early Years Foundation Stage (EYFS)	Foundation Stage	Curriculum for Excellence
Age range	3–7 years	Birth to 5 years	4–6 years	3–18 years
Areas of Learning	Seven areas of learning: Personal and Social Development, Well-being and Cultural Diversity; Language, Literacy and Communication; Mathematical Development; Welsh Language Development; Knowledge and Understanding of the World; Physical Development; Creative Development	Seven areas of learning: Prime areas: Communication and Language; Physical Development; Personal, Social and Emotional Development Specific areas: Literacy; Mathematics; Understanding the World; Expressive Arts and Design	Seven areas of learning: Religious Education; Language and Literacy; Mathematics and Numeracy; The Arts; The World Around Us; Personal Development and Mutual Understanding; Physical Development and Movement	Eight areas of learning: Expressive Arts; Health and Well-being; Languages; Mathematics; Religious and Moral Education; Sciences; Social Sciences; Technologies
Assessment	Teacher assessment of Foundation Phase outcomes at age 7 National Testing (Year 2)	Integrated Review at 2–2.5 years Assessment at the end of the EYFS – the Early Years Foundation Stage Profile (EYFSP)	Ongoing teacher assessment and observation; The Pupil Profile the statutory means of reporting to parents	Ongoing teacher assessment
Philosophy of Play	Learning through play is integral. Play should be planned for in an enabling environment with structured tasks implemented to support stages of development	The emphasis of the curriculum is through play, it must be planned for and purposeful. A mix of child led and adult led activities advocated	The majority of the learning children experience should be through well-planned and challenging play	Active learning which facilitates children's thinking using real-life and imaginary situations and play scenarios. Reggio Emilia approach also drawn upon

screening test at the end of Year 1 and SATs in Year 2. In Scotland, general screening takes place in P1 (Reception) to assess children's ability on starting school. There are standardised assessments in reading, maths and spelling every year from P2 (Year 2). In Wales, children take national Reading and Numeracy tests at Year 2; this has caused much controversy as to whether this is conducive to a play-based curriculum (Thomas and Lewis, 2016). In Northern Ireland, the biggest difference occurs with children being assessed every year through teacher assessment and planned tasks and activities rather than formalised tests.

A focus on the curriculum framework in Wales: The Foundation Phase

The Foundation Phase (Wales) is a play-based pedagogy; it is based on a holistic approach that encompasses a thematic, child-centred way of learning – theoretically children are taught at 'stage not age', however children are separated into year groups from Nursery to Year 2. There is an emphasis on outdoor learning and an experiential, hands-on exploratory methodology (WAG, 2008a). At the time of inception, the Foundation Phase framework was seen as a radical paradigm shift away from a more formal, didactic way of teaching to a curriculum that included both children's and adults' contribution to a shared learning experience (Waters, 2016). The Foundation Phase has seven Areas of Learning: Personal and Social Development; Well-being and Cultural Diversity; Language, Literacy and Communication Skills; Mathematical Development; Welsh Language Development; Knowledge and Understanding of the World; Physical Development; Creative Development (WAG, 2008a). It is based on what the child can do, generated by their prerequisites and tailored to suit their individual needs; it is not a 'deficit' model (WAG, 2008a).

Linking the Foundation Phase to theory

As well as drawing inspiration from international curricula, the Foundation Phase has evolved from a sound theoretical standpoint; traditional and contemporary theorists have had an influence on its conception. Vygotsky's social constructivist theory postulates a prominence on aspects of learning that require real-life experiential learning and the assumption that the quality of a child's social and cultural relationships is deemed crucial to their development (Gray and MacBlain, 2016). An enabling environment that encourages collaboration, sharing and joint problem-solving is also conducive to development. There is also a need for 'Focused Tasks' and specific teaching and learning activities facilitated by a qualified practitioner, the term that Vygotsky quantified as the 'Zone of Proximal Development' (ZPD) – the area of potential growth that is just beyond, yet in reach of, the child's current capabilities (Andrews, 2012). This requires facilitation and careful planning as well as observations of the child's stage of development. Children in Early Years settings do not develop solitarily; they learn from each other, through speaking, playing and imitating – coined by Vygotsky as from the 'More Knowledgeable Other' (MKO). This is exemplified in practice when children extend their own and others' play by adding extra resources, discussing possible outcomes, supporting, helping and creating imaginary scenarios with each other.

Likewise, Piaget's constructivist theory proposed that children were active participants who construct their own learning and consequently adults should create environments that support, facilitate and generate this (Crowley, 2017). Furthermore, although his work predominantly concentrated on cognitive growth and four stages of cognitive development (from the sensorimotor stage to the formal operational stage), he ascertained that play and natural discovery were essential components in this which would facilitate the development into a higher platform of learning where rules and more complicated systems could be applied (Whitebread, 2012). This is demonstrated in the Foundation Phase where the Continuous and Enhanced Provision are emphasised in the curriculum to allow for open-ended activities and more sustained periods of uninterrupted play and experiential learning.

Piaget (as well as other theorists such as Froebel, Steiner and Montessori) used the term 'schema' or 'schematic play' to encapsulate the cognitive and mental representation a child develops as they experience new concepts; it is repeatable actions that lead to logical systematic classifications and categories (Athey, 2007). Likewise, Bruce (2011) ascertains that schemas allow another perspective and an alternative view for practitioners to meet the child's individual learning needs. There are different types of schematic play that can be observed in Early Years settings: Transporting, Trajectory, Rotation, Connecting, Enclosing, Positioning, Enveloping and Orientation. An example of a 'Transporting schema' is a child who continually moves items from one place to another, e.g. carries blocks from the construction area into the role play area or carries sand into the water tray. However, as Thomas and Lewis (2016) highlight, there is very little reference made to schemas in Foundation Phase documentation and there appears to be minimal training available for Foundation Phase practitioners on this aspect of theory. In light of this many practitioners are not making the crucial links between schemas, enabling environments and the importance it has for holistic learning and development and, as exemplified by the 'Transporting schema', will often prevent and actively discourage children from doing this.

Influences of International Curricula – Reggio Emilia/Te Whāriki

The premise of play being integral to learning in Early Years is concurrent with all four curricula of the UK. Rhetoric, policy and pedagogy in this country do not appear in isolation; influences have been drawn upon from other international perspectives and this continues to evolve. Two approaches will now be briefly considered: the Reggio Emilia approach (Italy) and Te Whāriki (New Zealand), which both demonstrate elements that have been adopted by UK curricula.

The Reggio Emilia approach

This concept was founded by Loris Malaguzzi in 1963 following the assumption that a more innovative approach to learning was required post World War II to promote ethical and independent learners. This approach has accomplished international acknowledgment and the ethos and democratic pedagogy that are centred on child–adult engagement are respected in conjunction with the curriculum provision and the emphasis on creative arts (Wood, 2013). The emphasis of this approach is synonymous with a multimodal pedagogy and its 'One Hundred Languages of Children' tantamount to a stimulus to consider how children can be heard and how they can express themselves (Edwards et al., 2011). The empowerment of children is fostered in a creative way and learning is encouraged and facilitated through drawing, drama, music, painting and dance as well as play. The child is very much at the centre of this curriculum philosophy, with assessment and evaluation based on their needs. Children's work is primarily documented through photographs/videos, with the teacher adopting the role of researcher and their artwork (untouched by practitioners) is displayed with prominence in the settings (Luff, 2012). The environment is typified by a spacious and natural backdrop, with easy access to natural and recycled resources, often with mirrors to reflect light and promote a natural inquisition into perspective and form (Thornton and Brunton, 2007).

Parallels can be drawn with UK curricula, especially in regard to advocating a more holistic and thematic approach, viewing the child as central to the curriculum and the strong emphasis on the learner's individual needs. An enabling environment, the endorsement of learning through purposeful play and easy access to resources so that children can take a 'lead' in their own learning echo the Reggio approach. Also, the collaborative partnership emphasised by UK Early Years curricula between adults and children and the facilitation of experiential learning rather than an imparting of knowledge can be identified as a similarity (Soler and Miller, 2003).

In contrast, Wood (2013) emphasises that the Reggio model of delivery is steeped in the belief and overarching principles that are intrinsically bound by the communities and families that are involved. Likewise, Thomas and Lewis (2016) suggest that although practitioners in the UK may wish to advocate this philosophy, their attitudes and facilitation of creativity and play tend to have more dominance and control than the Atelierista (specialist art practitioner) in the Reggio approach. This is typified in UK settings particularly when the creative work of children is seen as formulaic or bound by rules of colour and shape, rather than a true representation of the child's self or work. Displays of children's painting can be extremely generic and are evidently not based on observation or a symbolic thought but rather the guidance, colours and instruction given by the practitioner.

The 'Te Whāriki' approach

The New Zealand perspective is metaphorically linked to the conceptualisation of the 'woven mat' or *whāriki* which is drawn from the principles (such as family/community and relationships), goals, learning outcomes and strands (e.g. belonging, well-being, communication) that are intrinsically connected (Wood, 2013). Concurrently, the importance of Māori tradition and cultural heritage is emphasised and adapted within different settings to reflect the multicultural society. Like the Reggio model, this approach places a heavy emphasis on building positive relationships with parents and the wider community. Practitioners working within the Early Years in New Zealand are required to have a comprehensive understanding of play and how it can be facilitated (Thomas and Lewis, 2016). Curriculum planning centres on the child, and learning wherever possible is based on their interests so that skills, knowledge and understanding can be embedded to reflect their holistic development (Andrews, 2012).

Echoes of this can be exemplified in UK curricula, where the acknowledgement of parents as the child's first educators is emphasised and the importance of play is advocated as well as a shift towards a more holistic/inclusive way of learning and teaching. This thematic approach to learning and cross-curricular planning is also evident in UK Early Years settings and comparisons can be drawn to the interweaving of the Te Whāriki principles and strands. Likewise, the increasing emphasis on the child's emotional well-being and cultural identity can be seen as an influence from this international curriculum (Soler and Miller, 2003).

However, the New Zealand approach to assessment is a significant difference from UK curricula. The Te Whāriki model measures achievement and attainment through 'learning stories' and not the summative learning goals, outcomes or performance indicators which are being adhered to in the UK. It could be argued that despite the shift in Early Years educational practices in the UK there is an inevitable modification in the practitioner's pedagogic response to one of planning to ensure they address curriculum requirements rather than supporting play from a child-led focus (Brooker, 2011). Invariably this has a significant implication for the pedagogy of play meeting imposed targets and measurable outcomes. Practitioners in New Zealand have far more autonomy in the teaching pedagogy they implement and the creative approach that they can 'weave' into their delivery. Arguably, UK curricula, due to the accountability in the assessment process, cannot advocate quite such a free approach to learning and some formal and discreet teaching of skills is standard practice. Despite the implementation issues discussed, the Te Whāriki curriculum and the Reggio model have developed international kudos and UK practitioners continue to aspire to the fundamental principles and elements of good practice that are advocated.

The role of the adult

Importance of planning – the what and why of planning

Effective learning and teaching does not occur accidentally, it has to be planned and prepared for in a robust way, whilst still retaining flexibility and responsiveness to children's needs (Wood, 2013). Every eventuality cannot be premeditated and children never cease to surprise practitioners in their responses and interpretations. It is of paramount importance therefore that the 'child's voice' is heard and incorporated into the planning process as there can be a mismatch between what teachers think they are providing and what the children think they have received (Brock, 2013). Moyles (2011) advocates that it is the role of the teacher to interpret the curriculum and skills that will enable progression and formulate these into learning activities for pupils in a creative and cross-curricular way. Wherever possible, planning by practitioners

(Continued)

(Continued)

should incorporate a cross-curricular approach to ensure that as many areas as possible are utilised without making tenuous links; learning does not occur in a compartmentalised, isolated way and the planning should reflect this. If play-based learning is planned for effectively, this can occur organically and provide maximum learning opportunities for children. This is endorsed and advocated by the Welsh Government, who indicate that play is so critically important to all children in their holistic development that society should seek every opportunity to support it and foster an environment that creates this (WAG, 2008b).

There are three types of plans:

Long-term plans – these generally demonstrate what will be taught over the whole year, with skills and routes of progression considered. This would concur with Continuous Provision. At this stage, all Areas of Learning need to be considered to ensure that there is not too much of an emphasis on one area and an overview of provision is considered. By setting up the learning environment to provide maximum learning opportunities and provision that is always available, such as sand and water, construction, dressing up/role play, painting, reading corner, writing/mark-making, clay/dough, outdoor area and ICT. The pupils can play independently following their own schema. This is vitally important to their individual development and allows the opportunity to practise, modify and problem solve in areas that are of interest.

Medium-term plans – these are typically for a term or half a term; they bridge the gap between the broad outline of the long-term plan and the day to-day detail of the short-term plan. Generally, a specific topic/theme is identified; this may incorporate a 'wow' factor to introduce it, such as a trip, a visitor, an ICT stimulus or some such exciting start that will engage and inspire the children at the outset. Ideally, pupils will be encouraged to be involved with this planning to ensure that their interests and lines of enquiry are considered. This type of planning is concurrent with Enhanced Provision. Some examples of themes/topics used in Early Years settings are 'Dinosaurs', 'People Who Help Us', 'Transport', 'Mini Beasts', 'Seaside', 'Growing', 'Seasons' and 'Ourselves'. Mind mapping is useful for practitioners at this stage to pool ideas, expertise and resources.

Short-term plans – these types of plans can be daily or weekly and incorporate the goals and objectives that have been set out in the medium-term planning as well as being driven by observing and assessing the children and continually adapting to suit their needs; it needs to be a working document with reflection at its heart. These types of plans require specific learning objectives, differentiation identified (how activities will be adapted for the varying levels of development), success criteria (how the objectives will be reached), resources required and the adult responsible; this type of planning links to Focused Tasks. This is primarily adult-led, whereby practitioners teach specific skills/concepts or knowledge to individuals or small groups of children. The learning is more directly measurable in this context, and the next steps can be identified.

Using the curriculum framework as a guide

Practitioners are required to employ the curriculum framework (in Wales, the Foundation Phase) to ensure that their planning is conducive to, and linked to, this document. Planning needs to encompass the seven Areas of Learning; although all areas need to be addressed to promote a broad and balanced curriculum. Personal and Social Development needs to be at the crux of all activities as children's well-being is now recognised as an essential component of effective learning (WAG, 2008a). Bryce-Clegg (2015) summarises this sentiment and highlights that children who feel positive, involved and engaged will ultimately learn more efficiently, and high-quality outcomes can be derived from settings that nurture well-being.

This Foundation Phase Framework (as revised 2015) can be found online (see Welsh Government, 2015).

Practitioners are required to utilise the *Range*, that gives an overview of the breadth of learning that needs to be addressed and decide what opportunities the pupils need to ensure this coverage (factors including socio-economic, EAL, SEN and the cohort of children also need to be considered at this stage). This Briggs and Hansen (2012) deem as 'personalising' or adapting to 'local needs' and ensuring that the curriculum is flexible and addresses the needs of pupils who attend the setting. In conjunction with this, the *Skills* stipulated also need to be addressed – so in simplistic terms the *Range* is the what and the *Skills* is the how. This, then, essentially gives the practitioner the autonomy to develop their plans in a creative and innovative way that draws upon their own strengths, motivation and interest as well as considering the collective and individual needs of their learners

(Moyles, 2011). Drawing upon this curriculum framework, practitioners then plan, in accordance with their setting's own approach, to ensure that the *Range* and *Skills* are met and are progressive across year groups. Planning should also evidence differentiation (catering for different abilities), opportunities for scheduled observations, key questions, pertinent lines of enquiry, open-ended questions and key terminology (Thomas and Lewis, 2016).

How is each stage of planning interlinked?

The three stages of planning (long-term, medium-term and short-term) do not operate in isolation; it is imperative for a curriculum framework to be effective so that learning and teaching are utilised concurrently – in simplistic terms that one leads on from the other (Envy and Walters, 2013). In relation to the Foundation Phase, the Focused Teaching element should not stand in isolation; the teaching that occurs at this stage needs to be reflected in the continuous and enhanced provision so that the children have the opportunity to consolidate and master skills. An example of how these three types of provision work together is illustrated in Table 2.2. The balance of Continuous and Enhanced Provision is currently ubiquitous debate amongst Early Years practitioners as they try to resist the powerful influence of over-intervention and regulations generated by inspection that create a detrimental influence over children's independent learning (Featherstone, 2014).

Table 2.2   An example of how the three areas of provision/planning are interlinked

Construction:	Areas of Learning from Foundation Phase Framework (2015):
	• Mathematical Development
	• Physical Development
	• Language, Literacy and Communication Skills
	• Personal and Social Development, Well-being and Cultural Diversity
Continuous Provision: *Long-term planning*	Construction area:
	Wooden blocks, hollow blocks, unit blocks (multilink), foam blocks, recycled blocks (e.g. telephone directories, milk cartons, cardboard boxes)
	Use of shadows and labels to aid with tidying up
	Ensure easy access to all resources
Enhanced Provision: *Medium-term planning*	To support and extend learning:
	Tape measure, measuring stick, string
	Hard hats, appropriate dressing up clothes
	Books and learning stories
	Pictures of a variety of buildings
	Prompt cards, labelling
	Large sheets of paper, sticky notes, pens, pencils
	Small world figures, people, cars, wild animals, dinosaurs, trains

Focused Teaching *Short-term planning* Work in small, differentiated groups	Mathematical Development: Compare blocks and objects made according to size, length and height. Use standard or non standard types of measurements (differentiation) Use positional vocabulary – over, under, beneath, above, below, inside, outside, behind, in front of Counting, one to one correspondence (touch counting) Physical Development: Develop fine motor skills Hand–eye coordination Balancing and placing Language Literacy and Communication Skills: Writing for a range of different purposes, e.g. signs, labels, instructions and explanation lists Describing what they are doing, giving instructions to others, listening to suggestions made by others Use a range of reading strategies to read signs, labels Use oral narration or writing/pictures to describe the journey of a small word figure, dinosaur or wild animal Personal and Social Development, Well-being and Cultural Diversity: Negotiate Take turns/share Appreciate the work of others in comparison to own Concentrate, persevere, take risks, explore possibilities *NB these are generic skills that could be covered and are not derived directly from the Foundation Phase Framework (2015)*
Role of the adult	• Observing children using the provision, to ascertain which items are being used, note roles adopted by the children, learning dispositions, key vocabulary heard, level of involvement, stage of development, how the area can be further enhanced • Help and aid children only when requested to by the child (unless Focused Teaching) • Ask open-ended questions (if the opportunity arises) • Encourage collaboration and sharing • Model tidying up • Positive behaviour management • Celebrate success

Case study

Case study: Sam

Sam is 3 years and 9 months; he attends a Nursery class five mornings a week. The short-term planning adopted in this practice changed the topic on a weekly basis. In week 1 the water tray had jugs and pipes

(Continued)

(Continued)

with connectors in. Sam spent a sustained period of time filling and pouring from the jugs and watching the water flow down the pipes. This play was observed daily over the course of the week, the same play being repeated again and again. The next week the focus of the planning had changed and the resources in the water tray were replaced with different materials (pebbles, small stones, shells and coloured water). Sam returned to the water tray and spent some time playing with the new resources. It was observed that he was not as engrossed in the activity as in week 1. At the commencement of week 3 the planning was modified again and the resources were replaced with fishing nets and pretend fish. It was observed that Sam did not play in the water tray that week.

Theory into practice

In the case study, whilst the practitioner's intentions were to stimulate interest and create new and exciting learning opportunities by changing the provision on a weekly basis, Sam's behaviour suggests that in week 1 he was utilising a 'Trajectory' schema (putting water in and out of containers) and this was interrupted in week 2. Sam was no longer able to repeat the actions that he so fervently adopted in week 1. By week 3 he had lost interest as the schema and learning behaviour he had adopted were not supported. Practitioners could have overcome this by ensuring that the Continuous Provision remained the same and that other resources were used as Enhanced Provision to ensure that children's individual schemas were recognised and encouraged. Likewise, his ZPD (Vygotsky, 1978) could have been addressed and pertinent questions asked, and further objects that support 'Trajectory' play introduced (e.g. saucepans, funnels, cylinders).

This notion is further corroborated by Moyles (1989), who suggests that the learning process that occurs when children are playing is like a spiral and is cyclical and recursive in nature. The process commences with exploratory play (free play) that the child has chosen, the second stage brings a degree of mastery as they continue to experiment, repeat and process concepts. This continues with structured or directed play (this is usually adult led or a focused task). Finally, this leads to an enriched free play as knowledge and abilities are acquired and consolidated. This spiral continues on and on as children go through these cycles many times with varied play experiences.

The emphasis in this model is on 'free play' and the time allowed to rehearse and consolidate learning at the child's own pace and at their developmental stage. Moyles (1989) advocates that first-hand explorations need to have occurred before adults should consider using material in a directed situation. Learning in a cyclical way is also conducive with Bruner's (1960) constructivist theory of the spiral curriculum, where concepts and ideas are structured so they are explored at a simplistic level initially, and revisited on numerous occasions to allow and facilitate more complex levels. This will allow children to develop skills to solve problems independently without always being guided by a teacher/practitioner. Both these concepts highlight imperative considerations for the role of the adult in children's learning and play, and the importance of Continuous and Enhanced Provision which forms the basis of the curriculum framework, whilst the focused teaching constitutes a smaller aspect.

In a recent evaluation, Siraj (2015) exemplified that a shift in emphasis of the workforce culture is urgently required, particularly in relation to the role of the adult in supporting learning and providing appropriate learning environments that foster play rather than viewing it as a contingency for when the child has finished their 'work'. This, in combination with her previous report (Siraj, 2014), strongly recommends a significant input into the professional development of those working in the Foundation Phase, as she indicates that the curriculum is being diluted in favour of a more didactic way of teaching and learning that has an emphasis on teaching skills and knowledge rather than learning through play. It is paramount that the child's conceptualisations are allowed the time, rehearsal in play and resources necessary to develop and that Early Years practitioners understand that learning does not always involve them directly.

Importance of observation and assessment

It is essential that the planning cycle in Early Years incorporates planned observations, assessment and reflection (Envy and Walters, 2013).

As depicted in Figure 2.1, each area of the cycle does not occur in isolation, assessment is an integral part of the learning and teaching process. By gathering information about a child's progress over a period of time, teachers build a comprehensive picture of the learning in order to plan future work (Wood, 2013). In all UK curricula, observing children is seen as a vital component of assessment, to allow practitioners to understand patterns of behaviour and notice developmental milestones; it can take the form of participant observation (entering the child's play world) or non-participant observation (detached from the event); both have a place in Early Years settings (Andrews, 2012). This type of formative (on-going) assessment can take different forms: tracking, sociogram, free description, time sample, event sample, checklist (WAG, 2008c). Whereas a summative

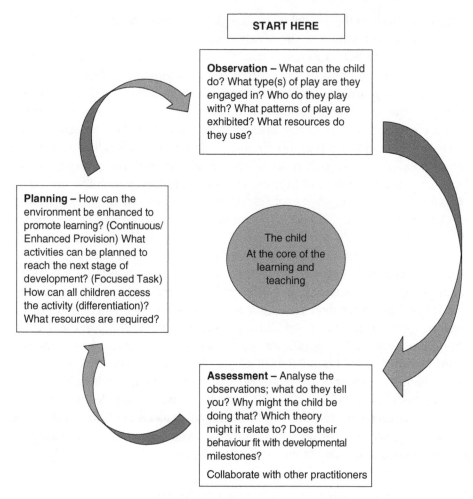

Figure 2.1   The planning cycle

assessment is usually typified by a formal report or test, this is also exempli-fied in UK curricula (generally at the end of the age phase) and illustrated in Table 2.1. Many Early Years' practitioners are opposed to this type of assessment as it can create a strain between an evidence-based curriculum and a focus on child-centred and child-led practice (Envy and Walters, 2013). This is exemplified in Wales, where much controversy surrounds the implementation of national testing at the age of 7 and is contrary to the practice of the Reggio and Te Whāriki approaches already examined, both of which place emphasis on the process of children's learning and develop-ment rather than on the end product such as a test (Thomas and Lewis, 2016). Assessment and the implications for effective practice are a significant factor for Early Years practitioners to consider; they should not be viewed as an 'add on' but should form part of the planning process as a whole. A very brief overview has been provided of the assessment process but further reading will be required to understand the complexity of this procedure.

Transitions and home–school links

It is imperative that a whole school approach is adopted for a smooth transition from an Early Years provision to Key Stage 2 (Foundation Phase, Wales) or Key Stage 1 (EYFS, England and Northern Ireland), otherwise attainment levels, behaviour and the well-being of the children will be affected. The shift from an experiential learning approach advocated in the Foundation Phase to a more traditional and content-based pedagogy at Key Stage 2 can be problematic. Morris et al. (2011) demonstrate that this can be overcome where primary schools strive to adopt a single philosophy of learning that underpins the two phases of learning and therefore facilitates an easier transition for staff to manage. Furthermore, practitioners across the phases need to work together and understand the implications of the curriculum demands; this can be achieved by allowing staff to experience both curricula (Rose, 2009). Cross-phase communication is essential to the process of aligning the two learning phases and effective monitoring of pupils' progress, and learning and teaching approaches need to be harmonised at the point of transition (Bryce-Clegg, 2015). Communication with parents and carers is also vital to ensure that they understand the difference between different curricula and what can be expected for and of their children at different school stages.

Questions for your practice

1. Why might some practitioners be opposed to a play-based curriculum? What implications does this have on the delivery of UK curricula based on this pedagogy?
2. How can you ensure assessment (both formative and summative) is included at the planning stage and why is this integral to effective learning and teaching?
3. Why is it so important that an enabling environment is established in Early Years settings and what impact does this have on pupils' learning experiences and their holistic development?

Summary

This chapter has highlighted the prerequisite for Early Years settings to implement a curriculum framework to ensure a consistency of approach that considers all areas of development and demonstrates cohesiveness amongst practitioners. The four UK curricula espouse a play-based curriculum for young children. Although each country has its own perspective and pedagogic basis, commonality between them is evidenced. It is essential for practitioners to have a secure knowledge of child development, appreciate the influence of theorists and consider international perspectives to their own practice. Practitioners need to work in a collegial way, ensuring that the child is at the centre of the learning. Whilst free play is important, careful planning (long-term, medium-term and short-term) is necessary to ensure that a wealth of learning opportunities are provided for young children and all areas of learning need to be considered so that a broad and balanced curriculum is in place. In addition, an enabling environment that is stimulating, challenging and planned for appropriately will ensure that young children are given the opportunity to rehearse and practise skills that will aid the transition to the next stage of development. The Foundation Phase (Wales) has been utilised as an example of how a curriculum framework operates in practice. Demonstrating how this curriculum functions in practice can be applied to other UK curricula as fundamentally the core principles are reciprocated in England, Northern Ireland and Scotland: adopting a thematic approach, the embodiment of holistic teaching and the implementation of the planning cycle (including observation and assessment). Curriculum frameworks are influenced by political and global agendas, they are continually changing and evolving, and do not stand in isolation from each other.

Recommendations for further reading

Bryce-Clegg, A. (2013) *Continuous Provision in the Early Years (Practitioner's Guide)*. London: Featherstone. In this accessible book creative and practical ideas that can be utilised to significantly enhance the enabling environment of the setting are demonstrated through photographs and real practice.

Nutbrown, C. (2011) *Threads of Thinking: Schemas and Young Children's Learning*, 4th edn. London: Sage. This is an essential read for practitioners working within Early Years – it explains the notions of schemas and why they are so important to developmental learning.

Thomas, A. and Lewis, A. (2016) *An Introduction to the Foundation Phase Early Years Curriculum in Wales*. London: Bloomsbury. There are many books on the EYFS but this book concentrates on the Foundation Phase in Wales. As well as drawing upon the pedagogy of this curriculum from its inception, it also guides practitioners on many aspects of practice that are applicable to any UK curriculum – methods of assessment, planning for purposeful play and reflective practice, for example.

References

Allen, S. and Whalley, M (2010) *Supporting Pedagogy and Practice in Early Years Settings*. Exeter: Learning Matters.

Andrews, M. (2012) *Exploring Play for Early Childhood Studies*. London: Sage.

Athey, C. (2007) *Extending Thought in Young Children*, 2nd edn. London: Paul Chapman.

Boyle, B. and Charles, M. (2016) *Curriculum Development*. London: Sage.

Briggs, M. and Hansen, A. (2012) *Play-Based Learning in the Primary School*. London: Sage.

Brock, A. (2013) *Perspectives on Play: Learning for Life*. Abingdon: Routledge.

Brooker, L. (2011) 'Taking play seriously', in S. Rogers, *Rethinking Play and Pedagogy in Early Childhood Education*. London: Routlege.

Bruce, T. (2011) *Early Childhood Education*, 4th edn. Abingdon: Hodder Education.

Bruner, J. (1960) *The Process of Education. A Landmark in Educational Theory*. Cambridge, MA: Harvard University Press.

Bryce-Clegg, A. (2015) *Best Practice in the Early Years*. London: Bloomsbury.

Cameron, C. (2006) *New Ways of Educating: Pedagogy and Children's Services*. London: Sage.

Crowley, K. (2017) *Child Development*, 2nd edn. London: Sage.

DfE (Department for Education) (2014) *Statutory Framework for the Early Years Foundation Stage: Setting the standards for learning, development and care for children from birth to five*. Available at: www.gov.uk/government/uploads/system/uploads/attachment_data/file/335504/EYFS_framework_from_1_September_2014__with_clarification_note.pdf (accessed 19 August 2016).

Education Scotland (2016) *Curriculum for Excellence*. Available at: www.education scotland.gov.uk/ (accessed 19 August 2016).

Edwards, C., Gandini, L. and Foreman, G. (2011) *The Hundred Languages of Children: The Reggio Emilia Experience in Transformation*. Santa Barbara, CA: Praeger.

Envy, R. and Walters, R. (2013) *Becoming a Practitioner in the Early Years*. London: Learning Matters.

Featherstone, S. (2014) *Learning to Learn*. London: Bloomsbury.

Gray, C. and MacBlain, S. (2016) *Learning Theories in Childhood*, 2nd edn. London: Sage.

Luff, P. (2012) 'Challenging assessment', in T. Papatheodorou and J. Moyles (eds), *Cross-Cultural Perspectives on Early Childhood*. London: Sage. pp. 140–50.

Morris, M., McCrindle, L., Cheung, J., Johnson, R., Pietikainen, A. and Smith, R. (2011) *Exploring Education Transitions for Pupils Aged 6 to 8 in Wales*. Cardiff: Welsh Assembly Government.

Moyles, J. (1989) *Just Playing? Role and Status of Play in Early Childhood Education*. Milton Keynes: Open University Press.

Moyles, J. (2011) *Beginning Teaching, Beginning Learning*, 4th edn. Maidenhead: Open University Press.

Palaiologou, I. (2016) *The Early Years Foundation Stage*, 3rd edn. London: Sage.

Rose, J. (2009) *Independent Review of the Primary Curriculum: Final Report*. Nottingham: Department for Children, Schools and Families.

Scottish Government (2013) *Play Strategy for Scotland*. Edinburgh: Scotland.

Siraj, I. (2014) *An Independent Stock Take of the Foundation Phase in Wales*. Cardiff: Welsh Government.

Siraj, I. (2015) 'Key findings from the Independent Stock Take of the Foundation Phase and evidence from research'. Keynote speech, *Children in Wales* Conference, Cardiff, 20 January.

Soler, J. and Miller, L. (2003) 'The struggle for early childhood curricula: A comparison of the English Foundation Stage curriculum, Te Whāriki and Reggio Emilia', *International Journal of Early Years Education*, 11 (1): 57–68.

Thomas, A. and Lewis, A. (2016) *An Introduction to the Foundation Phase Early Years Curriculum in Wales*. London: Bloomsbury.

Thornton, L. and Brunton, P. (2007) *Bringing the Reggio Approach to Your Early Years Practice*. Abingdon: Routledge

Vygotsky, L. (1978) *Mind in Society*. Cambridge, MA: Harvard University Press.

Waters, J. (2016) 'The Foundation Phase in Wales – time to grow up', *Wales Journal of Education*, 18 (1): 179–98.

WAG (Welsh Assembly Government) (2008a) *Foundation Phase Framework for Children Aged 3–7 Years in Wales*. Cardiff: DCELLS Welsh Assembly Government.

WAG (Welsh Assembly Government) (2008b) *Play Policy*. Cardiff: DECELLS Welsh Assembly Government.

WAG (Welsh Assembly Government) (2008c) *Observing Children*. Cardiff: DCELLS Welsh Assembly Government.

Welsh Government (2015) *Curriculum for Wales: Foundation Phase Framework* (revised 2015). Cardiff: Welsh Government. Available online at: http://gov.wales/docs/dcells/publications/150803-fp-framework-en.pdf.

Whitebread, D. (2012) *Developmental Psychology and Early Childhood Education*. London: Sage.

Wood, E. (2013) *Play and Learning and the Early Childhood Curriculum*, 3rd edn. London: Sage.

CHILD DEVELOPMENT IN PRACTICE

Karen McInnes and Holly Gallan

Reading this chapter will help you to understand and develop your knowledge of child development and to put this into practice. It is a vital that all those practitioners working with young children know about child development so that they can understand the developmental journey of the children they work with. This enables practitioners to:

- Fully understand the children they work with so they can plan appropriately for their development and learning
- Organise enjoyable and playful opportunities and experiences for children which maximise development and learning
- Observe and assess children appropriately, through play, starting from where the child is. From that starting point, they can identify children who might be struggling and need further assessment or intervention from other professionals
- Have meaningful conversations with parents about their children and parents can be confident in the knowledge that their children are entrusted to practitioners who know them
- Also have meaningful conversations with other professionals working with children, especially health professionals, with whom they need to liaise regarding children's progress

In order to develop understanding and knowledge of child development it is important for practitioners to be cognisant of developmental psychology and areas of child development. Child development is not the same as learning and areas of child development are different from areas of learning, and these distinctions are not always explained in curriculum guidance. In England in the Early Years Foundation Stage (EYFS) (DfE, 2014) this distinction is not made, whereas in Wales, in the Early Years Foundation Phase (EYFP) (Welsh Government, 2015), these terms are not used interchangeably. In this chapter these distinctions will be made. There will be discussion of the principles underpinning child development, theories of child development and areas of child development, including a discussion of attachment, a key aspect of children's development, which all practitioners need to be aware of. In addition, there will be discussion of observation and how observing children informs assessment of their development. Two case studies of children are used to support and exemplify practice in relation to child development alongside a third case study which is informed by the voices of practitioners who were interviewed regarding their knowledge and understanding of child development and how this works in their practice.

Key words

child development, attachment, stage theories, areas of development: motor, cognitive, social, emotional and moral

Theoretical perspectives

Child development

Development generally refers to changes, or patterns of changes, that occur over the life span (Berk, 2009; Crowley, 2017) and child development refers to those changes that occur within a specified timeframe, that of childhood, which is from conception to early adulthood, or 25 years of age (Keenan et al., 2016). Whilst learning overlaps with development, as both may refer to changes as a result of experience, learning also refers to changes that go beyond natural maturation and are a result of studying and teaching (*Oxford English Dictionary*, 2016). This is an important distinction to make, as although there may be times when it is appropriate to use the terms interchangeably there are times when they should not be. This is especially important in relation to Early Years curricula guidance. In the EYFS the two terms are generally used interchangeably, potentially giving the impression that Early Years practitioners can influence all learning and development. In the EYFP the terms are used separately and a distinction is made between moving children on in their learning but doing so when children are developmentally ready.

There are some Early Years commentators who take a critical stance towards child development as they view its scientific basis, Western bias and emphasis on linearity, with children developing in certain ways at certain times, as unhelpful for practice. It is seen as being one-dimensional and contributing to a deficit view of a poor child in need of intervention (Dahlberg et al., 2007). They argue that child development does not take into account the richness and complexity of children's lives and does not, therefore, provide an appropriate view of children. Studying Early Years curricula such as the EYFS and EYFP gives some credence to this view, whereby the curriculum is used to enable children to learn and develop and be measured against Early Learning Goals or Outcomes (DfE, 2015; Welsh Government, 2016).

However, whilst some of these criticisms may be valid, current writing on child development takes a broader and more holistic view and situates the child within a broader framework than just developmental stages at certain ages (e.g. Keenan et al., 2016; McDevitt and Ormrod, 2014). Current principles underpinning child development discuss the notion of 'contextualism'. This acknowledges contextual influences on development, such as biological, environmental, historical and cultural influences. It also takes into account unusual events that occur to an individual within their lifespan that might have an impact on a child's development, such as a major illness (Keenan et al., 2016). Another underpinning principle that is pertinent to child development and causes much debate is the nature versus nurture issue. This refers to whether development occurs due to the child's innate genetic inheritance or due to the surrounding environment and experiences of the child. As with all debates, extreme positions have been taken on either side to explain children's development. However, the most likely explanation is one that considers both sides and looks at the interaction between nature and nurture.

A final contentious issue is that of stage theories of development. These are where children are thought to progress through changes in development at certain ages and in certain ways. Some stage theories are thought to be hierarchical, with one stage laying the foundations for the next. Critics of child development find this issue particularly controversial, however, and there is considerable research evidence refuting the notion of rigid stage theories (McDevitt & Ormrod, 2014). Children develop at different rates and in different ways: one only has to think about the different ways children might crawl – on all fours or as bottom shufflers – and the different ages they might do this (Keenan et al., 2016). There are cultural differences as to when children learn to do things, for example children learning to walk at different ages depending on their cultural upbringing (Crowley, 2017). Today most contemporary developmental theorists would not support the notion of rigid stage theories (McDevitt and Ormrod, 2014). This is also reflected in the Early Years curriculum guidance. In both the EYFS and EYFP reference is made to the fact that children develop in different ways and at different rates. Understanding this is crucial for understanding children and to facilitate development (Tayler et al., 2015).

Theories of development

There are many theories of child development and these are often categorised differently in child development textbooks. The main theories are: biological, behaviourism and social learning, psychodynamic, cognitive-developmental, sociocultural and developmental systems (McDevitt and Ormrod, 2014). A very brief overview of each theory will be given:

- Biological theory – this focuses on nature and the inherited biological and physiological processes, including genetic inheritances, that influence development. It is concerned with the maturation of children both physically and in their abilities. Developmental charts and the notion of children reaching developmental milestones stem from this approach. Traditionally, this theory did not take into account children's experiences but contemporary theorists do take account of environmental experiences. Key proponents of this theory are Maria Montessori and Konrad Lorenz.
- Behaviourism and social learning theory – these are learning theories that emphasise nurture over nature. Behaviourism is concerned with learning as a result of external environmental stimuli and is the underlying theory behind behaviour modification programmes. This theory does not generally consider the role of underlying thought processes and emotion in behaviour. Social learning theory stresses the role of observation of behaviour and the resultant consequences and then modelling of others' behaviour for learning. Key theorists linked to behaviourism are B. F. Skinner and John B. Watson, with Albert Bandura being the main social learning theorist.

- Psychodynamic theory – this is focused on social and personality development and how internal drives and conflict influence these. Children's ability to express their feelings and resolve conflict is key to their emotional well-being and this theory underpins much therapeutic work with children. The most well-known theorists are Sigmund Freud and Erik Erikson.
- Cognitive-developmental theory – this theory looks at the changes in thinking and cognition which occur over time. It emphasises the active role children play in their development and how they learn from making sense of their experiences. Children are thought to develop through different stages as they mature, gradually becoming more logical and abstract in their thinking. It underpins a lot of current thinking in Early Years education, especially of young children, and Jean Piaget is the best-known theorist.
- Sociocultural theory – this theory also looks at changes in thinking but takes into account social and cultural influences on this development. A key aspect of this theory for Early Years practitioners is the idea of 'scaffolding' (Jerome Bruner) and how adults can facilitate children's learning. It is most often compared and contrasted with Piaget's cognitive-developmental theory. Lev Vygotsky changed thinking about Early Years education with this theory and with his idea of the 'Zone of Proximal Development' where children can attain with the help of a knowledgeable other.
- Developmental systems theory – this is an all-encompassing theory and looks at all the factors that influence children's development. These factors may come from a variety of systems surrounding the child, including the family, school, community and wider world. It is a dynamic theory and considers the two-way process that occurs between the child and the systems surrounding them. In this way risk and protective factors that may impact on development and learning can be recognised. Urie Bronfenbrenner developed this theory.

There is no one right theory. When looking at theories of development each one offers different insights and is open to criticism. Taking a pragmatic approach to utilising developmental theories is advised.

Areas of development

Textbooks may differ in their discussion, but the main areas of development would be considered as:

- motor development, including fine and gross motor skills
- cognitive development, including perception and language development
- emotional development, social development and moral development (Keenan et al., 2016).

These areas overlap with the areas of learning and development outlined in the EYFS and EYFP. However, there are differences, as both documents include Literacy, Mathematics, Understanding of the World and Expressive Arts and Design or Creative Development. In addition, the EYFP includes Welsh Language Development. These areas are not considered areas of development as such, but academic domains within development. To understand these aspects of development one needs knowledge of child development (McDevitt and Ormrod, 2014). For example, to understand a child's creative development one must have knowledge of cognitive development (how children think and represent the world) and physical development (a child's ability to hold pencils and crayons).

One aspect of development that is highly important for practitioners to understand is attachment, which is a part of emotional development. Without secure attachments children will not be able to develop and learn successfully (Rose et al., 2016). Attachment theory derives from the work of Bowlby (1969) and looks at how the relationship between a mother and baby has an impact on the child socially, psychologically and biologically. Practitioners may act as secondary attachment figures for children (Siegel, 2012) and this is the basis of the Key Worker system outlined in the EYFS. It is also important as any training standards related to working within an educational context with children make reference to knowing and understanding issues that may impact upon children's learning and development. Most recently, knowledge of attachment has been included in training standards for both Early Years and primary school teachers in England (DfE, 2016; National College for Teaching and Leadership, 2013).

The role of the adult

The role of the adult is an important one in relation to child development. The adult has the opportunity to influence the child's development through reinforcing desired behaviours with praise (behaviourism) or through modelling behaviour (social learning theory). By enabling the child to be active in their learning, their thinking can develop (cognitive-developmental theory). By talking and playing with the child the adult can influence development, especially cognitive and social development (sociocultural theory) and by listening to the child practitioners can understand the systems and processes around the child that influence development (developmental systems theory). In addition, by forming and sustaining playful relationships with children, and making them feel safe and secure, practitioners can foster attachment relationships that will enable development and learning. Finally, the beliefs practitioners have regarding children's development can have an impact on their practice, therefore a clear understanding of a child's developmental age and stage needs to be held to ensure there is not a mismatch between belief and practice (Salamon and Harrison, 2015).

Observation and assessment of development

A key aspect of the role of the adult is in relation to observation and assessment of development. Observation and assessment of children should occur through play. Play provides a natural opportunity to observe and document children's development. It offers a fear-free environment for observation and children are more likely to be performing to the best of their ability, therefore an accurate assessment of children's development can be made (Howard and McInnes, 2013). It must be remembered that it is not the role of Early Years practitioners to assess and diagnose developmental difficulties in children; however they are in a privileged position working with children for substantial amounts of time and getting to know them. Knowing about child development enables practitioners to spot any potential difficulties a child might be having and to liaise with parents and other professionals working with children to get support for the child.

There are many different types of observation: unstructured or participant observation, semi-structured observation and structured observation. Structured observations may be broken down further into: narrative observations, rating scales, checklists, sampling and diagrammatic (Palaiologou, 2016). All these observational methods have advantages and disadvantages (for a clear guide to the strengths and weaknesses of the different types of observation see Palaiologou, 2016: 96–9). The Early Years curricula guidance for both EYFS and EYFP make reference to the use of observation. The EYFS does not specify different types of observation but states that observation should be used to enable a practitioner to understand all aspects of development and that paper-work related to observation should be limited. The EYFP has a separate document related to observation (WAG, 2008). This is a helpful document which discusses the use of both planned and spontaneous observations, and itemises different ways of recording observations – for example, using sticky notes, diaries or record sheets, and useful questions that practitioners may ask themselves as they observe.

Many practitioners know about all these different types of observations but often use just one or two and some practitioners may not feel confident about observing and assessing children in relation to child development. There are many guides to child development tracking the progress of children in relation to development milestones (e.g. Sharma and Cockerill, 2014) and one guide to developmental milestones specifically related to play (Howard and Alderson, 2011). Using these guides alongside taking a range of observations of children will provide the best evidence base for understanding a child's development. However, it must be remembered that any developmental guide is only a guide; children develop at different rates, with some children taking longer than others to achieve the same milestone. Observation and assessment of a child's development should be considered holistically.

Case studies

Case study 1: Story time

Sam is a 3-year-old Looked After Child (due to chaotic family circumstances and abuse) in Nursery who has one-to-one support in the classroom. It is story time and Sam has been asked by the teacher to sit down with the other children to listen to the story. Sam stares at her, not sitting down, whilst the other children stare at Sam. Again, the teacher asks him to sit down like the other children. His helper kneels beside him and gently rubs his back encouraging him to listen to the story; she does not prompt him to sit down. The teacher starts to read and Sam stands looking at the book. He slowly edges towards the teacher to get a closer look at the pictures. The teacher again asks him to sit down. Sam turns and wanders off followed by his support worker.

Case Study 2: Free play time

Lucy is a 5-year-old in a Reception class. It is free play time and she is playing outside. She has set up a shop near to where a group of children are playing on trikes and bikes. She is the boss and her friend Nancy is her assistant. Lucy calls out to the children on the bikes to come over and buy their petrol and sweets from her shop. She is very persuasive and the children bike over. Nancy fills up their vehicles with petrol and Lucy serves them sweets and drinks. She tells them how much their purchases are and takes their money, counting change accurately from the till. She has a small notebook in which she writes out receipts using a mixture of well-formed letters and symbols. The class teacher is standing to the side writing a narrative observation of the play situation focusing on Lucy, who is her target child for the session. She writes down everything she can capture about the play situation. After school she completes a record sheet, ticking off aspects of Lucy's language, social, physical and cognitive development. She notes that Lucy is ahead of her peers on most aspects of development.

Case study 3: Understanding children's development

Interviews were conducted with four Early Years practitioners in Wales and England across the EYFP and EYFS. All the practitioners were female; one worked in Nursery, two in Reception and one in Years 1 and 2 (Years 1 and 2 are included in the Welsh Foundation Phase). All practitioners have a PGCE. The practitioners had varied knowledge of child development ranging from 'I possibly did training linked to child development in college or for my GCSE Psychology but that was a long time ago' (Practitioner 4) to 'I think having children has informed me more about child development than my PGCE' (Practitioner 2). All the practitioners were clear that 'child development is how children develop in their lives' (Practitioner 3) and that 'there are different stages that children should reach by different ages' (Practitioner 1), however, as she goes on to say, there will be a 'difference in time scales in which children reach those aims, hopefully

(Continued)

(Continued)

all children will reach them, but some will reach them much quicker than others'. Knowledge of areas of child development was mixed and often confused with academic areas of learning from their respective curriculum documents as stated previously, whilst others had a very narrow view of child development. The practitioners had not studied anything about attachment: 'I haven't done any reading or been on any courses about attachment but I think a basic insight would be useful' (Practitioner 2). All the practitioners recognised the importance of the role of the adult in relation to child development and attachment. As Practitioner 3 stated, 'children do develop at their own rate but this is not something that can be abandoned or put on hold. Child development needs to be nurtured in order for the child to flourish to their full potential'. Observation was mentioned by all the practitioners as being important to understand and assess children's development, although some practitioners mentioned other ways to track their development: 'I track children's development though observations, listening to learners, testing, formative assessments, summative assessments, looking at books and talking to staff members' (Practitioner 1). Observation of child development was also seen as a key way to identify those children having difficulties: 'with such a diverse range of abilities, I treat milestones as a guide, but any red flags in terms of not meeting expected milestones help to possibly identify SEN [Special Educational Needs]' (Practitioner 4).

Theory into practice

Child development

The in-depth study of children's development is a part of many undergraduate disciplines of study, such as psychology, childhood studies and degrees related to health, like speech and language therapy for example. It is also a part of many Early Years practitioners' training, such as nursery nurse training, but it is not necessarily a part of teacher training. Therefore, it is not inconceivable that some Early Years practitioners will not have a detailed understanding of how children develop. This is unhelpful, as Doherty and Hughes (2014) state that it is necessary to have an understanding and appreciation of child development theories in order to develop professional practice.

Case study 1 above exemplifies this varied understanding. The teacher's expectations of Sam's behaviour could be considered unrealistic. Many 3-year-old children find it hard to sit and listen to a story but may listen standing up. In addition, bearing in mind his background as a Looked After Child having experienced family trauma, expecting him to sit down with a group of children was unrealistic. His one-to-one support worker had a clearer understanding of his development and needs, and her approach, to get down to his level and allow him to listen whilst standing up, was more appropriate. Case study 2 demonstrated that the Early Years practitioner was using her knowledge of child development to observe and assess the child's development. What is unknown from the observation is the basis for the statement that Lucy is ahead of her peers in most areas of child development. Careful cross-referencing of evidence from the observation with texts on child development should be undertaken to verify this. The practitioners interviewed for this chapter had differing knowledge of child development and theory. This mixed knowledge is not surprising considering the limited training received by practitioners.

Use of child development theory was evident in Case study 1 as the one-to-one support worker employed social learning theory by modelling sitting and listening. She might also have drawn on knowledge of psychodynamic theory when recognising his feelings and letting him wander away when the situation became too difficult for him. In that particular case study, drawing on developmental systems theory would have been helpful to the teacher in understanding his situation and anticipating his possible reactions. This might have made the situation more manageable with a different outcome to the one that occurred. In Case study 2 the Early Years practitioner was using knowledge of biological theory, cognitive-developmental theory and sociocultural theory as she observed Lucy at play and made sense of her observations. In Case study 3 when asked about theories of child development very little was mentioned and most of the practitioners stated that further training and courses on child development would be welcomed.

Attachment

Case study 1 was focused on a child with attachment difficulties, and knowledge of not only child development but also attachment should have guided expectations and interactions with this child. From the case study it was clear that this knowledge was missing from the teacher in her expectation that Sam would sit down amongst a group of children and listen to a story. The one-to-one support worker demonstrated her understanding of attachment by not expecting him to necessarily sit down and listen and also by her attempt to help him self-regulate his emotion by gently rubbing his back.

As previously discussed, it is important that Early Years practitioners know and understand about attachment, but knowledge and understanding between the four practitioners were scant. However, one practitioner had been on an Emotion Coaching course since qualifying and had a detailed knowledge of attachment. Emotion Coaching is a strategy that can help create an enabling environment for emotional well-being by fostering nurturing relationships (Rose et al., 2016). This is achieved by focusing on the emotions underpinning behaviour and working with children so they can self-regulate. This practitioner understood how a child with attachment difficulties might present in the classroom and felt she could respond appropriately. Amongst the others, training would be welcomed in this area.

The role of the adult

Case studies 1 and 2 demonstrated the many and varied role of the adult in relation to child development. In Case study 1 the one-to-one support worker observed and supported Sam to listen to a story amongst a group of children. She used her knowledge of child development to not expect him to sit down and her knowledge of attachment to help him self-regulate, something children with attachment difficulties find hard to do. She also used her knowledge of theory to model expected behaviours. In Case study 2 the practitioner stood back from the play and observed. Again she used her knowledge of child development and theory to assess Lucy.

From Case study 3 it is clear that the practitioners have a clear view that the role of the adult is important in this area. An Early Years practitioner is pivotal to the development of children in their care. In addition, developing a relationship with children was seen as vital to achieving this; getting to know children as individuals and forming relationships with them was seen as a crucial part of the job. The benefits of a play-based curriculum and playful relationship were also recognised as key to a child's development and again the role of the adult was paramount. Taking opportunities to play and develop a respectful dialogue with children and build positive and strong relationships was seen as fundamental to forming an attachment relationship with a child and thereby ensuring a sound basis for emotional well-being (Rose et al., 2016).

Observation and assessment

In Case study 1 participant observation was used by the one-to-one support worker as she observed and worked with Sam to help him listen to the story. Assessment was 'in the moment' as she knelt beside him and rubbed his back, judging that he needed support with self-regulation and that this might enable him to stay and listen to the story, which he was clearly interested in, for longer. In Case study 2 the Early Years practitioner was using non-participant observation as she stood to the side of the play situation and conducted a narrative observation. In this observation she was writing down everything that occurred; describing the play situation and writing everything that was said and done. This is a difficult type of observation to conduct but one that offers a rich and complete picture of the situation (Palaiologou, 2016). Using the observation to assess Lucy, by ticking off developmental behaviours on a pre-prepared checklist, provides an overview of Lucy's development but this is only a snapshot and does not provide a rationale or complex picture of her development. In addition, making judgemental statements in relation to developmental levels based on this type of assessment, with limited reference to theory, can be problematic. However, this detailed evidence can be used to improve outcomes (Tayler et al., 2015).

The importance of observation is evidenced by the practitioners in Case study 3. For practitioners in Wales, they have a particular mode of assessment called 'Incerts' (www.assessmentfoundation.org). This is an assessment tool based on the Welsh National Curriculum and it also has links with child development, in terms of Foundation Phase outcomes that link to educationally expected norms. It is used as an on-going tracker which informs the next steps of learning and planning. However, this highlights the criticisms of child development being used within Early Years practice as the use of developmental tick-lists results in a narrow, linear and deficit view of the child, with areas of development achieved and others highlighted that might need further intervention (Dahlberg et al., 2007).

However, in accordance with contemporary child development theory (e.g. Keenan et al., 2016) the four practitioners recognised that milestones or 'norms' should be treated with caution and that there was natural wide variance in rates of development. The practitioners did state that knowledge of child development and assessment and identification of SEN could ensure that children could be referred to appropriate agencies for further advice and help.

Transitions and home–school links

It was felt by practitioners that child development was used more in the Foundation Phase, which in Wales, as stated earlier, means for children up to the end of Year 2: 'I think it may be used more in the Foundation Phase compared to Key Stage 2' (Practitioner 3). It was also recognised that understanding child development enabled practitioners to have a view of the whole child rather than compartmentalise the child into academic areas of learning: 'I think in the Foundation Phase the focus is more holistic, focusing on every element of child development, including reading and writing but also how they eat their lunch' (Practitioner 1).

There was acknowledgment though that all teachers would probably know something about child development but it was maybe not reflected in practice in the later years: 'I think all teachers will have an understanding of child development but I think teachers in the Foundation Stage would perhaps have a more in-depth understanding, especially of the lower developmental norms because as the children get older you expect them to be able to do the lower developmental norms and they may forget that child development comes into teaching' (Practitioner 2). However, the importance of the Foundation Years was seen as crucial to future development: 'The Foundation Phase is often the first educational experience for a child. If a child has a positive experience during their Foundation Phase years, their school life is much more likely to be a continued positive experience, with the child developing crucial social and emotional skills as well as progressing academically' (Practitioner 4).

Understanding about child development is seen as useful as a means to talk with parents about their children, although it is dependent upon the parent and their wishes. Curricula guidance, both within the EYFS and EYFP, states that parents should be informed about their child's development with some statutory reporting, for example the integrated review at age 2 to 2·6 years within the EYFS. In relation to child development theory and Bronfenbrenner's developmental systems theory, this knowledge is in-built to using the theory. This is exemplified in Case study 1, as to work appropriately with Sam and facilitate his development knowledge of his background, including family history and current family circumstances, is paramount. Knowledge of child development is also important at parents' evening and when talking with parents (Reynolds and Duff, 2016). Parents know when they are talking to a practitioner who knows their child. Being able to talk meaningfully and appropriately about a child develops trust in the practitioner–parent relationship, which fosters home–school links.

Supporting child development in your practice

From the current curricula guidance, literature on child development and case studies there are messages that can help practitioners in their practice to support child development. These are:

- Read and refer to child development texts and checklists to ensure that observations and reflections are appropriate to the age and developmental stage of the child. Using curricula guidance only is insufficient (Tayler et al., 2015).
- Take a holistic view of the child and child development and understand one's own expectations in relation to children's development (Salamon and Harrison, 2015).
- Understand the impact of the wider context on children's development and involve the family in your developing understanding of a child's development (Reynolds and Duff, 2016).
- Purposefully and appropriately use a wide range of observational methods and tools to enable understanding of children's development (Palaiologou, 2016).
- Provide a language-rich environment with opportunities to develop playful and supportive relationships with children that foster attachment and development (Rose et al., 2016; Tayler et al., 2015).
- When appropriate, liaise with health professionals to support children who are struggling in their development.

Questions for your practice

[1] What is your knowledge and understanding of child development, where has it come from and what further training would enable you to develop your knowledge and understanding?
[2] What observational methods and tools do you currently use in your practice and how might you develop your observation skills?
[3] How do you currently work with parents and carers in relation to understanding a child's development? What more could you do?

Summary

This chapter has provided an overview of theories and areas of child development and it has highlighted some contested aspects of the use of child development within Early Years practice. It has provided a brief overview of attachment theory and discussed how knowledge and understanding of attachment theory are vital in work with children. It has used case studies of children and the voices of practitioners to demonstrate how child development is used in practice. It has shown how there is variation in the knowledge and understanding practitioners have in relation to child development but they understand its importance. The same can be said for knowledge and understanding of attachment. Practitioners use their knowledge of child development to observe and assess children and to plan for their learning. Practitioners need to consider the wider context around the child in order to understand and explain a child's development. It is also recognised that knowledge and understanding of children and how they develop are crucial to effective Early Years practice and getting this right provides a secure foundation for children's future development. To this end some guidance has been provided for practitioners to develop their practice and support children's development.

Recommendations for further reading

Crowley, K. (2017) *Child Development. A Practical Introduction*, 2nd edn. London: Sage. This text links theory and practice and includes some chapters not usually encountered in texts on child development, such as play. The new edition has an open access Companion Website with lots of resources.

Palaiologou, I. (2016) *Child Observation*. London: Sage. A clearly written and in-depth guide to observation.

Reynolds, B. and Duff, K. (2016) 'Families' perceptions of early childhood educators' fostering conversations and connections by sharing children's learning through pedagogical documentation', *Education 3–13*, 44 (1): 93–100. Based on research conducted in Australia, this journal article looks at how sharing documentation concerning children's development aids home–school links.

Rose, J., Gilbert, L. and Richards, V. (2016) *Health and Well-being in Early Childhood*. London: Sage. A clear and detailed introduction to the theory of attachment, neuroscience and how to implement this knowledge in practice through Emotion Coaching.

References

Assessment Foundation (n.d.) Incerts. [Online] Available from: www.assessment foundation.org/about-incerts.html?lang=en (accessed 12 May 2017).

Berk, L. E. (2009) *Child Development*. London: Pearson/Allyn & Bacon.

Bowlby, J. (1969) *Attachment and Loss*, Vol. 1. New York: Basic Books.

Crowley, K. (2017) *Child Development: A Practical Introduction*, 2nd edn. London: Sage.

Dahlberg, G., Moss, P. and Pence, A. (2007) *Beyond Quality in Early Childhood Education and Care: Languages and Evaluation*. London: Routledge.

DfE (Department for Education) (2014) *Statutory Framework for the Early Years Foundation Stage: Setting the standards for learning, development and care for children from birth to five*. Available at: www.gov.uk/government/uploads/system/uploads/attachment_data/file/335504/EYFS_framework_from_1_September_2014_with_clarification_note.pdf (accessed 12 June 2016).

DfE (Department for Education) (2015) *Early Years Foundation Stage Profile*. Available at: www.gov.uk/government/publications/early-years-foundation-stage-profile-handbook (accessed 12 June 2016).

DfE (Department for Education) (2016) *A Framework of Core Content for Initial Teacher Training (ITT)*. Available at: www.gov.uk/government/uploads/system/uploads/attachment_data/file/536890/Framework_Report_11_July_2016_Final.pdf (accessed 22 June 2016).

Doherty, J. and Hughes, M. (2014) *Child Development Theory and Practice*. Harlow: Pearson.

Howard, J. and Alderson, D. (2011) *Play in Early Childhood: From Birth to Six Years*. London: Routledge.

Howard, J. and McInnes, K. (2013) *The Essence of Play*. Abingdon: Routledge.

Keenan, T., Evans, S. and Crowley, K. (2016) *An Introduction to Child Development*. London: Sage.

McDevitt, T. M. and Ormrod, J. E. (2014) *Child Development and Education*. Harlow: Pearson.

National College for Teaching and Leadership (2013) *Teachers' Standards (Early Years)*. [Online] Available from: www.gov.uk/government/uploads/system/uploads/attachment_data/file/211646/Early_Years_Teachers__Standards.pdf (accessed 12 June 2016).

Oxford English Dictionary (2016) Oxford University Press. [Online] www.oed.com/view/Entry/106723?redirectedFrom=learning#eid (accessed 23 June 2016).

Palaiologou, I. (2016) *Child Observation*. London: Sage.

Reynolds, B. and Duff, K. (2016) 'Families' perceptions of early childhood educators' fostering conversations and connections by sharing children's learning through pedagogical documentation', *Education 3–13*, 44 (1): 93–100.

Rose, J., Gilbert, L. and Richards, V. (2016) *Health and Well-being in Early Childhood*. London: Sage.

Salamon, A. and Harrison, L. (2015) 'Early childhood educators' conceptions of infants' capabilities: The nexus between beliefs and practices', *Early Years: An International Journal of Research and Development*, 35 (3): 273–88.

Sharma, A. and Cockerill, H. (2014) *Mary Sheridan's From Birth to Five Years*. London: Routledge.

Siegel, D. (2012) *The Developing Mind: How Relationships and the Brain Interact to Shape Who We Are*. New York: The Guilford Press.

Tayler, C., Cloney, D. and Niklas, F. (2015) 'A bird in the hand: Understanding the trajectories of development of young children and the need for action to improve outcomes', *Australasian Journal of Early Childhood*, 40 (3): 51–60.

WAG (Welsh Assembly Government) (2008) *Observing Children*. Cardiff: Welsh Assembly Government.

Welsh Government (2015) *Curriculum for Wales: Foundation Phase Framework (revised 2015)*. http://gov.wales/docs/dcells/publications/150803-fp-framework-en.pdf (accessed 12 June 2016).

Welsh Government (2016) *Early Years Outcomes Framework*. http://gov.wales/docs/dcells/publications/150916-early-years-outcomes-framework-en.pdf (accessed 12 June 2016).

PLAY AND PLAYFULNESS: THE FOUNDATION OF LEARNING AND DEVELOPMENT

Karen McInnes and Natacha Yuen

Reading this chapter will help you to understand the value of play and playfulness as a foundation for learning and development in the Early Years. It will highlight the value of differentiating between play and play-fulness and argue how both should be taken into account when teaching young children. It will also demonstrate how playful educators are required to form playful relationships with children and engage in playful teaching to provide the foundation for effective learning and development. The importance of play for Early Years education is rarely disputed and its value has been referred to as the 'idealisation of play' (Sutton-Smith and Kelly-Byrne, 1984). However, its worth is rarely discussed outside the con-fines of Early Years education and its value within the primary phase of education generally goes unacknowledged. The chapter will draw on two case studies: one focused on brick play and one entitled 'The Monster', both taken from an English Children's Centre and featuring children aged 3–4 years. The case studies will be used to demonstrate what play and playfulness means in practice in relation to both the Early Years Foundation Stage (EYFS) (DfE, 2014) and Early Years Foundation Phase (EYFP) (Welsh Government, 2015), how theory links with practice and how a sensitive and playful practitioner may facilitate play and playfulness across the primary phase. Both these documents:

- Make the case for play for learning and development, however the EYFP identifies the value of play for the primary phase, up to 7 years of age, not just the early years of education.
- Value the role of play and first-hand experience for children's learning and development. Within the EYFS this is exemplified through the three characteristics of effective teaching and learning: playing and exploring, active learning and creating and thinking critically. Within the EYFP this is conveyed through words such as 'first-hand experiential activities', 'experimenting' and 'risk-taking'. This document is also original in stating that play can be a serious endeavour for children and, in this chapter, this is shown during the brick play case study.
- Extol the value of play for children's learning with the EYFP stating that play is crucial to learning and the EYFS stating that it is essential for learning. This stance is debated in the literature although it is acknowledged that play is important for learning and development and should be supported (Smith, 2010).

Key words

play, playfulness, children's view of play, choice, control, relationships, environment

Theoretical perspectives

Play and playfulness

Historically, play has been seen as the only mode of education for young children and play has underpinned early childhood programmes since the initial kindergarten developed by Froebel (1782–1852). This tradition has continued, albeit in different guises, through the work of pioneers in early childhood education such as Montessori (1869–1952), McMillan (1860–1931) and Isaacs (1885–1948). Today, play is promoted in the Early Years through the EYFS, which applies to children aged 0–5 years. In this document it is planned, purposeful play and adult-led as well as child-led activities which are promoted, rather than the free play originally promoted by the pioneers of education in the early years. In Wales, the EYFP covers the age range 3–7 years, which encompasses the early years of education as well as part of the primary phase covered by the National Curriculum in England. Within this document it is also stated that children should learn through the provision of both child-initiated and adult-initiated activities; however, the types of play that children need to engage in are not clearly stated.

There are many theories as to why children play, including: play being a form of recreation, play as a re-creation of human evolution, play as a behaviourally conditioned response to others and play as a cultural activity to identify with and learn about one's culture (Edwards, 2012). Within an educational context play has traditionally been seen as a vehicle for learning and this is the underpinning theoretical stance as to why children play that is communicated in the EYFS and EYFP, even being overtly stated in the EYFP. However, many theorists and commentators of play today would view play from a much broader perspective and argue that this should be the case within education (Edwards, 2012; Fleer, 2013; Howard and McInnes, 2013; Moyles, 2012; Wood, 2013). Post-developmental and post-structuralist theories of play provide different and broader ways of thinking about play. They are less concerned with the why of play but focus on problematising play and understanding its complexity as children engage in and experience different types of play (Fleer, 2013). This way of theorising play potentially offers the practitioner an alternative means to gain a deeper understanding of children's play. In essence, children play for a variety of reasons that all contribute to their learning and development. Understanding and drawing on different theories of play should inform educational play practice with children and open up possibilities for play in the classroom alongside playful interactions with children that facilitate learning and development.

As well as there being many theories about why children play, there are many ways to define what play is. Play has been defined according to category. Piaget (1951) devised a developmental categorisation of play which aligned with his stages of intellectual development: practice play, occurring between birth and 2 years of age; symbolic play, occurring between 2 and 7 years of age; and games with rules occurring from 7 years of age. Coming from an emotional perspective, Erikson (1963) devised a developmental framework of play focusing on developing a sense of positive self-esteem and competence. His stages aligned with the first three stages of his psychosocial stages of development and with Piaget's play stages, albeit having a different focus. He names his stages: autocosmic, concerned with sensory and physical play; microspheric, focused on object play; and macrospheric, to do with pretend and role play. Finally, in relation to stage theories, Parten (1932) devised a developmental stage framework of social play from birth to 6 years-plus based on her observations of children's play. She stated that there were six stages of social play from unoccupied behaviour, which was children not playing but observing others playing, to cooperative play whereby children play together with shared intentions about the play. As with all stage theories these may be critiqued, as children do not progress through discrete stages, they often do these at different ages to the ones stated and the stages do not cover all types of play. Criteria definitions of play (e.g. Rubin et al., 1983) focus on behaviours and dispositions of play and the criteria include: positive affect (happiness), choice, intrinsic motivation (motivated by internal rewards) and pretence (make believe). Using these criteria, observers of play can determine how like play an activity is. However, some criteria are less observable than others, for example intrinsic motivation, and although some types of play (for example, role play) can obviously be determined as play, other types of play, such as playing with jigsaws, are less obvious. Play types are another way of defining play. Again, these are based on observable behaviours that children display when they play and so are open to the same critique as the criteria definitions of play. Types of play include: creative play, rough and tumble play and object play (Hughes, 2006). Bruce (1991) argued for a different type of play called 'free flow play' whereby children would become immersed in their play.

However, it is debatable how much these definitions are helpful to practitioners and Moyles (1989) argues that play is impossible to define. One reason for it being impossible to define, and therefore unhelpful to practitioners, is that it means different things to different people (Howard, 2002). It has been argued that play should be viewed from the individual player's perspective (Howard and McInnes, 2013; Sutton-Smith, 1997). Viewed from this perspective, play can then be defined as a form of communication, a stance taken when play is utilised for therapeutic purposes and is seen as the basis from which to establish a positive relationship (Landreth, 2012). Understanding play according to children's views and seeing play as communication and the bedrock of the practitioner–child relationship may be considered helpful to practitioners as they engage in, and facilitate, children's play experiences.

Viewing play from children's perspectives has not been traditional practice within education where the focus has been on providing planned play opportunities or adult-initiated activities and where child-initiated activities have been ones where the adult is potentially responsive to the play or absent (Edwards, 2012; Wood, 2013). This model of play practice has contributed to differing views of play between adults and children (Howard and McInnes, 2013). Adults have traditionally viewed play according to the definitions above. These have all focused on the observable play act. Research investigating children's views of play has consistently shown differences with adult views of play. Children use cues such as: location, choice, locus of control (who is in control), adult presence, positive affect and adult evaluation to determine between play and not-play activities. Play activities are more likely to be ones that occur on the floor, where children have choice and control, when an adult is not present, when there is positive affect and when there is no adult evaluation. Not-play activities are more likely to be ones that occur at a table, where children have no choice or control, when an adult is present, when there is negative affect and when there is adult evaluation of the activity or the product from the activity (Howard and McInnes, 2013). Recent research has indicated that within a Welsh context, where the EYFP is implemented, these cues are also used by children up to 7 years of age (Owen-Leeds, 2012). In relation to development, further research has demonstrated that when children are provided with activities that fulfil their criteria of play they are enabled to feel playful and show enhanced learning and well-being (Howard and McInnes, 2012; McInnes et al., 2009; Thomas et al., 2006).

It has been argued that listening and acting on children's views of play enables playfulness (Howard and McInnes, 2013). Playfulness has been viewed as an approach or attitude that is taken towards an activity. It comprises of affective qualities, such as pleasure, involvement, motivation, concentration and enthusiasm, and qualities that are considered to be most important for development and learning (Moyles, 1989). In fact, it has been argued that playfulness is so important that it may eventually be considered more important than the play act itself (Bundy, 1993). In addition, the research demonstrating enhanced learning and well-being would appear to support this notion as in these studies children in the playful practice conditions displayed the affective qualities associated with playfulness. Many of these qualities are also described by the EYFP in their discussion of qualities necessary for learning through play. So, it may be suggested that the act of play itself is less important than providing an environment based on children's views of play which facilitates playfulness.

The role of the adult

The environment provided for play also includes the adult, and adult beliefs about play and the way they interact with children may also encourage playfulness and facilitate learning and development. Practitioners who are playful themselves, secure in their understanding of play theories, acknowledge children's views of play and provide children with a sense of control and choice, and offer a situation where they are less likely to use the cue of adult presence. Practitioners also need to provide children with time and space to play. Children need to be provided with a variety of open-ended resources that can accommodate their play needs. They need space, which enables them to move around in their play and have a sense of freedom. Depending on the activity, this does not have to be a big space; squatting or lying on the floor whilst playing with bricks does not take up a lot of space. Practitioners who can provide this physical and emotional environment for play are more likely to be invited into children's play as co-players engaging in playful interactions that facilitate learning and development (McInnes et al., 2011; McInnes et al., 2013).

This way of facilitating play takes us back to the idea of viewing play as a form of communication and using it as the basis to form a positive relationship with children. Theoretically, this is the bedrock of play therapy practice (Landreth, 2012; West, 1996) and, whilst educational practitioners are not therapeutic practitioners, drawing on additional theoretical perspectives that can aid us in our practice can be beneficial. Developing a positive relationship is fundamental to play therapy practice and it has been demonstrated that teachers who know a little about play therapy practice have more effective teacher–child interactions (Hsu-Smith, 2009). Therefore, borrowing ideas from that alternative practice base, a positive relationship should be developed by basing it on understanding play from children's perspectives alongside being knowledgeable regarding the wide theory base underpinning all play. It means viewing play as a form of communication and working with children's cues of play to provide an environment that fosters playfulness and is centred on playful encounters with children. Playful encounters require respect and security alongside time and space to play and understand one another. It also means that during verbal and non-verbal communication control and choice are shared to maximise playfulness, learning and development.

Case studies

Case study 1: 'The Monster'

Grace rushes in

G: Anna [teacher], there's a monster outside and he's chasing us.
Anna: A monster?! ...
G: Yes, an Oliver monster.

Grace rushes back outside to Tobias.

G: So where's that bad guy?
T: Bad guy ...?
G: He's there in our classroom – quick let's tell Anna.
T: Tell Anna ...

They rush in and Grace puts her hands on her hips.

G: You know there's a monster outside. I saw one over there ...
        let's go get him then you're not sad.

She says this to Charlie, who has been finding it hard to separate from
his mother that morning. She runs outside and Charlie follows.
    Two minutes later they come back in.

T: [*very excited*] The bad guys they hitted me and then I hitted
        them and put them in jail.
Anna: You hit them and put them in jail ...?
G: Yes and I cut their heads off ... the bad guys.
Anna: [*smiling*] It sounds like you're the bad guy, Grace, cutting their
        heads off.
G: [*looks puzzled*] I'm not the bad guy.
Anna: But if you're hurting people maybe that makes you a bad
        guy.
G: [*thinks for a moment*] Well anyway, they are in jail.

Case study 2: Brick play

Anna (teacher) is seated on the carpet with a range of different blocks
around her. Different children have been coming and going but two

(Continued)

(Continued)

girls (Aneesha and Lacey) have stayed with her for about half an hour or so, one on each side of her and each building individual models. Both girls are leaning into Anna, possibly looking for physical closeness, and keep tapping her if she turns her attention elsewhere.

A: I have made soft play. [*Waits for Anna to look and acknowledge her.*] Tom the cat is hiding.

She places a small toy cat under some blocks.

Anna: That is Tom from home. You often bring him in. I wonder why he's hiding ...?

A: [*whispers*] Quiet.

Aleesha brings the cat out from under the bricks and makes it bounce on some of the coloured blocks, whispering under her breath and looking frequently to Anna. Meanwhile Anna turns to the other child, Lacey. She has stood two long blocks on end and put another smaller one inside

L: Look, Anna, that's elebator ...

Anna: That's your elevator going uuuuuuup... [The blocks all fall over.] Oh no, the elevator made your tower fall down.

Lacey repeats standing the blocks up and making them fall down, tugging at or touching Anna each time.

   Anna turns to a child (Dakarai) behind her. 'Builded house' he says, when he sees Anna looking.

   Lacey is tapping Anna, wanting to continue with her game.

Anna: Let's look at Dakarai's house.

Lacey moves over to look but gets no response from Dakarai, who remains engrossed in his play. Lacey turns to look at Aneesha's model.

Anna: That's a good idea. We can look at Aneesha's soft play. Where has Tom gone?

Lacey tugs at Anna to return to their original game.

> *Anna:* Lacey, I am going to play with Aneesha for a minute and you could help us. We could help her build her soft play.
> *A:*   I don't want Lacey help.
>
> Lacey quietly knocks Aleesha's model down as soon as Anna looks away and Aleesha's eyes fill with tears. She does not say anything, holds on to her toy cat and puts a block in Anna's hand to show she wants help. Anna clears a space so that Aleesha can build her model without disturbance.

Theory into practice

The case studies

In this section we look at how the case studies demonstrate the way play theory links with practice and how learning within the Early Years curricula frameworks can be achieved. In Case study 1, The Monster, we see children engaging in free flow play, a type of play described by Bruce (1991) where children are engaged in play that is initiated by them and they own it. Children are playing in an enabling environment, one advocated by the pioneers of Early Years education such as Froebel, where they can play freely indoors and outdoors, moving securely between the two areas. In terms of children's perspectives of play, this is play; they are in control and have chosen the play, they are outside and not constrained by furniture and they are choosing to involve the adult, Anna. They invite Anna into their play and are secure that she will accept and respect their highly imaginative play about the monster that is outside. This she does by responding to their language and ensuring that she understands the play scenario. She is respectful and enters the play on their terms and accepts the imagined violence within the play. She is playful with them, smiling whilst she jokes with Grace about her role in the play, and provokes a different way for Grace to think about the play thus causing her to look puzzled. However, Grace is safe and secure in her relationship with Anna and knows that she is in control and does not have to accept this alternative viewpoint and consequently chooses to ignore it.

In terms of the EYFS, despite this not being planned play, the three characteristics of effective teaching and learning are demonstrated:

- The children in the scenario are playing and exploring, they are engaged in active learning and they are creating and thinking having had an idea for a play scenario and having had the freedom and a playful adult to enable them to develop their idea.
- The children are engaged in learning related to communication and language; they are speaking with one another and they are speaking with an adult. They are also developing their vocabulary, using words such as 'jail' correctly and using both present and past tenses. They show awareness of the listener, providing Anna with the necessary information to understand and join in their play. They are also able to respond to 'what … if' when Anna presents them with an alternative point of view. They have constructed a playful narrative that makes sense to all players. They are engaged in physical development being physically active as they rush between inside and outside.
- They are also demonstrating personal, social and emotional development as they play with one another and invite the adult into their play. In addition, they show sensitivity to another child, who has been finding it hard to separate from his parent, inviting him into their play.
- Finally, their story shows their ability to engage in expressive arts and be imaginative.

In the EYFP, play is frequently discussed as occurring in small groups and this play scenario is small group play with members of the group changing; initially starting with two players, then three and then the addition of the adult. According to the EYFP the areas of the curriculum encountered during this play episode are: language and communication, personal and social development and physical development.

In Case study 2, Brick play, the serious business of play is demonstrated as discussed in the EYFP. In this play scenario, the play is less active and energetic than in the first case study but this does not make it any less playful. The play shows children concentrating and paying attention to detail as well as creating imaginative worlds. The children are inside playing with bricks while sitting on the floor and as we join the play they have been engaged in the activity for at least half an hour. Many adults, less knowledgeable about young children, will claim that they are not capable of concentrating for extended periods of time but, when engaged in playful activities of their own choosing, children are capable of proving these commentators wrong.

- Again, according to children's perspectives of play, this is a play activity; they have chosen it, are in control, on the floor and have an adult play partner beside them. The adult is invited into the play and playfully joins each child in their play at their level, checking with each one that she understands the play. There is a close and positive relationship between the children and Anna, the teacher, both physically and emotionally. Each child keeps close to her and is safe and secure knowing that they can get her attention both physically and verbally. Anna sensitively encourages the children to join in with each other's play; however this does not work out, and although upsetting for one child this is handled with the minimum of fuss and play continues. Once again the sometimes serious nature of play is demonstrated. In terms of the curriculum many areas of the EYFP are covered. Personal and social development and well-being are displayed as the children can ask for help and can communicate what is right and wrong although it is evident that further learning is needed in this area in terms of others' perspectives. They are engaged in physical development, not the gross motor active play of the first case study but fine motor development as they build with bricks. The children are engaged in communication and developing their language as they communicate with the adult both verbally and non-verbally. They are able to express themselves appropriately, are extending their vocabulary through the use of words such as 'elevator' and show a pragmatic understanding of language, whispering when saying 'quiet'. Through the act of building they are grappling with mathematical concepts of shape and space.

Again the three characteristics of effective teaching and learning from the EYFS are shown. As with the first case study this is not a planned, purposeful play activity; rather it is a purposeful child-initiated play activity. In accordance with the EYFP, the areas of learning of the EYFS covered in this case study are: personal, social and emotional development, language and communication, physical development and mathematics. A different interpretation of creativity within the EYFS, which is called expressive arts and design, means this area of the curriculum is covered through being imaginative and telling stories.

Play and playfulness

Both case studies demonstrate the type of free play envisaged by the pioneers of Early Years education such as Froebel. It is not the planned, purposeful play initiated by adults as described in the EYFS and EYFP but rather the child-initiated play also described in the two documents. Why are these children playing in the ways described in the case studies? There are probably various reasons for their play: it seems to be fun, at least in the monster play and most of the brick play. Their play may be considered as recreation or a release of energy or physical development or as a vehicle for learning (Edwards, 2012); in fact it may be considered under many of the theoretical perspectives proposed across time. In may be helpful to consider it through the lenses of post-developmental and post-structuralist theories of play (Fleer, 2013). In the first case study we can use Schousboe's (2012, cited in Fleer, 2013) spheres of play to analyse how the children create an imaginary situation, re-enact roles within the situation and how children are still connected to reality, as Grace considers the proposition that she might be a bad guy but ultimately rejects it. In the second case study we can use post-structuralist views of play to interrogate the end of the scenario when Lacey knocks over Aneesha's model and ask questions to understand what this play interaction might mean for both Lacey and Aneesha and how Anna, the teacher, might develop her play practice.

Both case studies demonstrate the difficulty of trying to describe what play is. According to Piaget's (1951) play categories, practice play, symbolic play and games with rules are all demonstrated despite the fact that the children are all of a similar age, 3–4 years of age. Likewise, the same can be said for Erikson's (1963) play categories. In relation to Parten's (1932) social play categories we can possibly see cooperative play being demonstrated in the first case study as the children are playing with a shared intention. In the second case study we can see both solitary play, as the children are generally playing by themselves, but also parallel play, as they are playing the same type of activity alongside one another. Often when we observe play scenarios we can see children moving between different play categories within the same play frame. Using the play criteria we can see that in the first case study children are demonstrating pretence, positive affect, choice and motivation: we can call it play. However, in the second case study, whilst the children have choice and are motivated, there is less pretence and at the end an absence of positive affect. Does this make it less like play? According to proponents of play criteria it would be, but according to children that would be unlikely. We could also examine the types of play being displayed, however different typologies of play would define them differently. Is the first case study showing imaginative play, fantasy play or social play? Is the second showing imaginative play, constructive play or creative play and does it matter? What probably matters is what the children believe. According to children's perspectives both case studies constitute play. Both scenarios are playful encounters whereby the children have choice, they are in control, they are not constrained within their location and the adult is included in the play as a true play partner.

The role of the adult

In both case studies, Anna, the teacher, has carefully observed and listened to the children so that she understands the children and their play before entering it. She queries, 'a monster?!' in the monster play to ensure that she knows what the play is about, what the children are running from. She waits for children to speak to her about their play, 'I have made soft play' or 'builded house', before she talks with them about their play and she asks questions to understand their play rather than presuming she knows, 'I wonder why he's hiding ...?' She accepts the children and their play. She accepts their emotions when they are excited at the possibility of a monster chasing them and them hitting the monster and putting it in jail. In the second case study, she accepts and respects that the children do not want to help each other with their soft play, as when Lacey knocks down Aneesha's model to demonstrate her wish to not help. She then sensitively accepts Aneesha's sadness and helps her move on. She accepts the boisterousness of the play in the first case study as they rush about and she accepts the aggression in the play as they talk about cutting off the monster's head.

   Both case studies are playful encounters. They both demonstrate those affective qualities associated with taking a playful approach to an activity: pleasure, involvement, motivation, concentration and enthusiasm. Anna contributes to that by being playful herself. She smiles at the children to encourage them, she poses playful questions, 'it sounds like you're the bad guy', and playfully exaggerates her speech, 'that's your elevator going uuuuuuuup...'. She also provides the children with a safe and secure environment. She is there for them, providing a place of safety as they keep running in and out in the monster play, and she is close by to the children as they need to engage with her physically during the brick play. Overall, this is viewing play as a form of communication and using it to offer and develop a positive relationship. Observing, listening, being accepting and respectful enable Anna to understand the play. She waits to be invited into the play and then ensures she understands before entering the play and then playfully interacts with the children whilst providing them with the safety and security to explore the play they have created.

(Continued)

(Continued)

The adult's role is to also create an environment that fosters play. In this setting the children have the freedom to move indoors and outdoors. They are also able to play in a variety of ways and can move furniture and resources around to suit their play creations. They are provided with space and time to immerse themselves in their play and, as shown in Case study 2, they can play for long periods of time without interruption. The children are given a choice to play where and how they would like and to create endless play scenarios; they are in control and that is respected. They are provided with resources that offer them possibilities and they are offered experiences that build upon their interests. Overall, the adult and environment facilitate play and playfulness.

Transitions and home–school links

The EYFP is designed for children aged 3–7 years with a requirement that these children learn through first-hand experiential activities. Play is considered to be the vehicle for learning right across Years 1 and 2. This is not the case for children in England moving between the EYFS and the National Curriculum, however organising activities that children are more likely to view as play and therefore playful, and having teachers and children engaging in playful encounters, is not impossible. Children can still have a mix of practitioner-initiated and child-initiated activities and within both types of activities they can be afforded choice and control. For example, allowing children to choose types of paper, writing implements and subject matter during a writing activity enables them to have some control over the activity. Allowing children choice over where an activity takes place can enable an activity to feel more play-like; sitting on the floor rather than at a table can make a huge difference in terms of their perspectives of play. Small changes such as those suggested above will enable children to view an activity as more like play and foster playfulness and, as research suggests, this will aid learning and well-being (Howard and McInnes, 2012; McInnes et al., 2009; Thomas et al., 2006).

Thinking about play as a form of communication and the basis for positive relationships with children is helpful and should be a part of the role of a practitioner. Being playful will foster playful encounters and this can be achieved by talking to children about their play and their activities. Accepting them and what they tell you will show that you value play and enable a relationship to develop. Practitioners need to be playful with children and, whilst this might sound easy, being playful whilst facing the demands of a room full of children is difficult. Smiling, laughing and joking when appropriate will demonstrate your playfulness. Asking children playful, open-ended questions and questions to make them think and ask further questions will promote playfulness and learning. Play and playfulness foster deep learning and are achievable beyond the early years of education.

Play starts in the home and it is important that practitioners are knowledgeable about children's play histories and their play likes and dislikes. This can help them in their endeavour to understand the play they observe in the setting and to view and use play as a form of communication. They need to talk with parents and carers about children's play at home and in the setting so that there is shared understanding about play and how children are developing and learning through their play. Misunderstanding about the value of play by parents and carers once their children enter educational establishments is common (Fung and Cheng, 2012) and so this dialogue is vital. This dialogue is also important to aid the transition between home and school for young children. It is also important for children to see that their play at home is valued. This provides important messages concerned with respect and acceptance which are crucial when forming positive relationships with children. One obvious way of achieving this is to allow children to bring toys from home, as exemplified in Case study 2, where Aneesha is playing with her toy cat, Tom, and Anna acknowledges this by stating, 'That is Tom from home. You often bring him in'.

Questions for your practice

[1] How could you develop your play practice to enable children to feel playful?
[2] How playful do you think you are and what steps could you take to enable more playful encounters with the children in your setting?
[3] How could you cultivate a dialogue between all practitioners within your setting to develop a shared understanding of play and playfulness to maximise the learning potential of all children?

Summary

This chapter has summarised many theoretical perspectives concerning play and provided practitioners with an alternative view of play, one from children's perspectives which also enables it to be seen as a form of communication. It has also demonstrated that seeing play through the eyes of children, the players, can provide an insight into playfulness and differentiating between the act of play and a playful attitude or approach may be more useful to practitioners. It has shown how using play as a form of communication, enabling children to be playful and being a playful practitioner can result in playful encounters that foster positive relationships between practitioners and children. In turn, this fosters learning and development. This way of viewing and using play and playfulness can be translated into practice with children both within the early years of education and beyond.

Recommendations for further reading

Edwards, M. (2012) *Exploring Play for Early Childhood Studies*. London: Sage. This text takes a wide perspective on play and provides the reader with a good overview of the subject.

Fleer, M. (2013) *Play in the Early Years*. Melbourne: Cambridge University Press. This text takes an historical-cultural view of play and introduces the reader to contemporary theories related to play.

Howard, J. and McInnes, K. (2013) *The Essence of Play*. Abingdon: Routledge. This takes a wide-ranging look at play from different professional standpoints.

References

Bruce, T. (1991) *Time to Play in Early Childhood Education*. London: Hodder Stoughton.

Bundy, A. C. (1993) 'Assessment of play and leisure: Delineation of the problem', *American Journal of Occupational Therapy*, 47 (3): 217–22.

DfE (Department for Education) (2014) *Statutory Framework for the Early Years Foundation Stage: Setting the standards for learning, development and care for children from birth to five*. Available at: www.gov.uk/government/uploads/system/

uploads/attachment_data/file/335504/EYFS_framework_from_1_September_2014_
with_clarification_note.pdf (accessed 28 April 2017).

Edwards, M. (2012) *Exploring Play for Early Childhood Studies*. London: Sage.

Erikson, E. H. (1963) *Childhood and Society*, 2nd edn. New York: W. W. Norton.

Fleer, M. (2013) *Play in the Early Years*. Melbourne: Cambridge University Press.

Fung, C. K. H. and Cheng, D. P. W. (2012) 'Consensus or dissensus? Stakeholders'
views on the role of play in learning', *Early Years*, 32 (1): 17–34.

Howard, J. (2002) 'Eliciting young children's perceptions of play, work and learning
using the activity apperception story procedure', *Early Child Development and
Care*, 172: 489–502.

Howard, J. and McInnes, K. (2012) 'The impact of children's perceptions of an
activity as play rather than not play on emotional well-being', *Child: Care,
Health and Development*, 6 June. doi: 10.1111?j.1365-2214.2012.01405.x.

Howard, J. and McInnes, K. (2013) *The Essence of Play*. Abingdon: Routledge.

Hsu-Smith, T. (2009) 'Echoing teachers' voices: A study exploring teachers' perceptions of play, play therapy, and play therapy skills training', PhD Dissertation,
The University of Texas at Austin.

Hughes, B. (2006) *Play Types: Speculations and Possibilities*. London: Centre for
Playwork, Education and Training.

Landreth, G. L. (2012) *Play Therapy. The Art of the Relationship*, 3rd edn. London:
Routledge.

McInnes, K., Howard, J., Miles, G. and Crowley, K. (2009) 'Behavioural differences
exhibited by children when practising a task under formal and playful conditions', *Educational & Child Psychology*, 26 (2): 31–9.

McInnes, K., Howard, J., Miles, G. and Crowley, K. (2011) 'Differences in practitioners' understanding of play and how this influences pedagogy and children's
perceptions of play', *Early Years: An International Journal of Research and
Development*, 31 (2): 121–33.

McInnes, K., Howard, J., Crowley, K. and Miles, G. (2013) 'The nature of adult–
child interaction in the early years classroom: Implications for children's perceptions of play and subsequent learning behaviour', *European Early Childhood
Education Research Journal*, 21 (2): 268–82.

Moyles, J. (1989) *Just Playing? Role and Status of Play in Early Childhood Education*.
Milton Keynes: Open University Press.

Moyles, J. (2012) *A to Z of Play in Early Childhood*. Maidenhead: Open University
Press.

Owen-Leeds, S. (2012) 'Understanding older children's perceptions of play and
subsequently manipulating the cues: The effectiveness of playful practice for
problem-solving', Unpublished Dissertation, University of Glamorgan.

Parten, M. (1932) 'Social participation among preschool children', *Journal of
Abnormal and Social Psychology*, 28 (3): 136–47.

Piaget, J. (1951) *Play, Dreams and Imitation in Childhood*. London: William
Heinemann.

Rubin, K. H., Fein, G. G. and Vandenberg, B. (1983) 'Play', in P. H. Mussen (ed.),
Handbook of Child Psychology, 4th edn. *Vol IV: Socialisation, Personality and
Social Development*. New York: John Wiley & Sons. pp. 694–759.

Smith, P. K. (2010) *Children and Play.* Oxford: Wiley–Blackwell.

Sutton-Smith, B. (1997) *The Ambiguity of Play.* Cambridge, MA: Harvard University Press.

Sutton-Smith, B. and Kelly-Byrne, D. (1984) 'The idealization of play', in P. K. Smith (ed.), *Play in Animals and Humans.* Oxford: Basil Blackwell. pp. 305–21.

Thomas, L., Howard, J. and Miles, G. (2006) 'The effectiveness of playful practice for learning in the early years', *Psychology of Education Review*, 30 (1): 52–8.

Welsh Government (2015) *Curriculum for Wales: Foundation Phase Framework (revised 2015).* http://gov.wales/docs/dcells/publications/150803-fp-framework-en.pdf (accessed 3 May 2017).

West, J. (1996) *Child Centred Play Therapy*, 2nd edn. London: Hodder Arnold.

Wood, E. (2013) *Play, Learning and the Early Childhood Curriculum.* London: Sage.

UNDERSTANDING WELL-BEING IN THE EARLY YEARS

Alyson Lewis and Lucy Rees

Reading this chapter will help you to understand the various meanings associated with the concept of well-being as well as the different dimensions, such as 'objective' well-being which mainly relates to statistics, and 'subjective' well-being which relates to someone's feelings. Well-being is generally understood as a 'catch-all' concept that encompasses many different aspects of a child's life (Amerijckx and Humblet, 2014). However, there is not always consensus about its meaning for children (Statham and Chase, 2010) and Gasper (2010) suggests that well-being constitutes fuzzy components. In addition to a lack of consensus about child well-being, there is very limited research that focuses on understanding the meaning of well-being regarding the curriculum, pedagogy and assessment (Davis et al., 2010; Soutter et al., 2012). Therefore, this chapter explores how well-being can be promoted and supported by drawing upon two case studies from an Early Years Foundation Stage (EYFS) Reception class.

Despite a lack of consensus and research, well-being is an appealing concept, particularly at policy level (Amerijckx and Humblet, 2014), and in the last decade or so there has been a fast-growing interest in children's well-being, particularly in education (Coleman, 2009). For example, Every Child Matters identified children's 'economic' well-being as one of its five outcomes. In 2008, 'Personal and Social Development, Well-being and Cultural Diversity' became an area of learning in the Foundation

Phase in Wales. However, the way in which child well-being is assessed has not kept pace with the development of adult well-being measures (Fraillon, 2004). Therefore, this chapter:

- Explores some of the ways in which children's well-being can be captured
- Discusses some of the challenges associated with capturing children's well-being

Key words

well-being, objective, subjective, domains, pedagogy, play

Theoretical perspectives

Multiple meanings

The concept of well-being is traditionally rooted within philosophy, psychology and economics, therefore many different explanations and definitions are in use. Clack (2012) suggests that, to some extent, the various perspectives are all underpinned by happiness but the way in which happiness is understood varies. For example, there is often a debate about whether well-being and happiness are related or fundamentally the same concept. Table 5.1 identifies some of the different theories of well-being which are discussed in more detail in the case studies:

Martin Seligman (2011; cited in Dodge et al., 2012), a well-respected positive psychologist, suggests that well-being is about **P**ositive emotion,

Table 5.1 Different theories of well-being

Philosophy	Psychology	Economics
Hedonism/mental states: happiness	Affect (positive and negative emotions)	Capabilities approach: contexts, interactions and relationships
Eudaimonism/flourishing: having a sense of purpose in life	Life satisfaction/cognitive evaluation of life	Gross Domestic Product (GDP) indicator as a measure for well-being (proxy measure)
Needs-based/objectivist list theory: underlying conditions		
Desire-based/preference satisfaction		

Engagement, Relationships, Meaning and Accomplishment (PERMA). However, Roberts (2010) claims that well-being consists of four themes: physical development, communication, belonging, and boundaries and agency and these four themes are discussed in more detail in one of the case studies.

Well-being dimensions

Generally, well-being is broadly understood as having two dimensions, namely the 'objective' and the 'subjective', and both dimensions are considered to be complex in nature (Mayr and Ulich, 1999; Dodge et al., 2012). The objective dimension is usually understood as a concept that can be quantified and tends to have a fixed meaning. Dodge et al. (2012) draw upon Reber's (1995) definition of well-being which is rooted more in psychology than philosophy, claiming that well-being is a state of being stable. Their definition includes psychological, social and physical resources that support a stable state of well-being.

Mashford-Scott et al. (2012) refer to the objective dimension in the context of Early Years as the developmental-oriented view and describe well-being in the form of indicators such as children's achievements, skills and abilities. Statistics about attainment, school attendance and free school meal data are often used as indicators of well-being. These are known as proxy measures, so for example when you cannot measure exactly what you want/need you measure what you can. However, one of the drawbacks of relying on objective indicators is that assumptions can be made about children's well-being when they have not been directly consulted themselves (subjective well-being).

In contrast, the subjective dimension tends to have an unfixed meaning and is associated with someone's feelings and their experiences which fluctuates and varies according to aspects such as: age, gender, status, place, culture (Ereaut and Whiting, 2008). Mashford-Scott et al. (2012) describe the subjective dimension in the early years as being more child-centred and focusing on a child's sense of well-being which involves intrinsic feelings (Mashford-Scott et al., 2012). Waters (2009) describes the subjective dimension as the holistic perspective of well-being which relates to children's lived experiences and a notion of feeling valued. The subjective dimension is not usually associated with young children and one reason for this is that some practitioners take it for granted that young children have a limited ability to make a valuable contribution.

The subjective dimension is closely associated with values where someone reflects on and considers what is important to them (Gasper, 2010).

Gasper (2010) suggests that well-being is not a single thing or a concept that can be easily defined. He further argues that well-being is about a broader, philosophical concept of being human. Similarly, Ereaut and Whiting (2008) claim that well-being is about the aspects that make up a good life. These views suggest that defining well-being is problematic and establishing its meaning is challenging (Coleman, 2009; Statham and Chase, 2010), particularly for young children. Deciding on what makes a good life for children is open to much debate.

Well-being domains (types)

Sometimes, when researchers write about well-being they clearly state what they mean and the following two examples show this. For example, Edwards et al. (2015) refer to well-being in terms of body weight and obesity, whereas when Taylor et al. (2015) write about well-being they state it is about a measure of 'pupil' well-being and 'physical' well-being. The two examples show that well-being has two different meanings in the context of research. Also, the description by Taylor et al. (2015) refers to different domains, also known as types of well-being, namely 'pupil' well-being and 'physical' well-being, which indicates that well-being is recognised as a concept that encompasses different domains. Another example of a domain is evident in the Every Child Matters (ECM) agenda which includes 'economic' well-being as one of its five outcomes (Thompson and Marks, 2006).

Some research about the domains of children's well-being under the age of 8 years was done in 2009 by Fauth and Thompson (2009) who conducted a review of well-being for the National Children's Bureau. They identified the following four domains:

[1] physical well-being,
[2] mental health, emotional and social well-being,
[3] cognitive and language development and school performance
[4] beliefs

However, in 2010 Statham and Chase (2010) reported that child well-being usually relates to three broad domains, and identified the following:

[1] emotional well-being
[2] physical well-being
[3] social well-being

This highlights a lack of consensus about well-being domains for young children.

The role of the adult

Well-being and the curriculum

In the last two decades, well-being has been presented to practitioners in different ways in curriculum policy. For example, in 1996 Wales and England introduced its first statutory Early Years curriculum for 3-to-5-year-olds called the 'Desirable Outcomes', and presented well-being as a 'principle of good quality educational practice'. It placed an expectation on practitioners to take responsibility for children's general well-being (ACCAC, 2000) but it was not an area of learning. Then with the introduction of the Foundation Phase in Wales in 2008, well-being was positioned in the one of seven areas of learning called 'Personal and Social Development, Well-being and Cultural Diversity'. The direction for implementing this area is 'integrated' across the curriculum whereas non-statutory guidance provides mixed messages and suggests that practitioners can teach the area discretely or integrate it across the curriculum. In relation to the EYFS, well-being is not explicitly included as an area of learning but 'general' well-being is mentioned. Well-being also appears in the child protection section. This highlights that different understandings of well-being exist in curriculum policy in England and Wales.

Pedagogical approaches

According to the Organisation for Economic Co-operation and Development (OECD) (2006) two pedagogical approaches are beneficial for children's well-being. Firstly, they state that adults should recognise children's agency and respect every child's way of learning. Secondly, practitioners should engage with a pedagogy of listening and fully embrace project work. We argue that a child's natural learning strategy would involve 'play' of some sort. According to Woolf (2013), play helps children develop self-awareness and self-confidence and it provides them with opportunities to develop social skills and learn how to cope with their feelings.

However, Gleave and Cole-Hamilton (2012) highlight that it is difficult to provide a causal link between play and well-being which is often the case between well-being and education. Mashford-Scott et al. (2012) suggest that in order to best support children's well-being, practitioners need to begin to understand how children experience subjective well-being and find out the factors that contribute to their well-being.

Seland et al. (2015) set out to explore in what contexts 1-to-3-year-olds experience subjective well-being. They found that when practitioners are very sensitive and responsive to children's needs and create equitable spaces; this promotes children's well-being. The findings from Seland et al.'s (2015) study show that children experience subjective well-being when adults, firstly, view children as subjects of their experience and focus on the here and now as in *beings*, rather than focusing on the future as in *becomings*. Secondly, children are more likely to experience subjective well-being when practitioners enact a rights-based pedagogy. Another recent study conducted about young children's well-being in education found that when practitioners engage with children's interests, their learning is more meaningful as opposed to focusing on interventions that modify children's behaviour (Edwards et al., 2015).

Intervention programmes

Research evidence about children's well-being mainly relates to specific targeted intervention programmes, such as the Student Assist Programme (SAP) and the Social and Emotional Aspects of Learning (SEAL) programme, but the evidence is mixed and there is dispute over what can be achieved in the long term (Humphrey et al., 2010).

Recent reports on children's mental health are over-pessimistic and overstated argue Ecclestone and Hayes (2009a), and this has led to an increase in intervention programmes (Ecclestone and Hayes, 2009b). They further argue that the debate about therapeutic interventions has largely been uncritical and it promotes an image of the child as vulnerable, needy, weak and fragile. Conversely, Bartholomew (2007) argues that when there is evidence that intervention programmes work, children should not be denied the intervention. According to Durlak and Weissberg (2013) there are endless controlled research studies that show that social and emotional programmes can make a difference and improve children's academic outcomes. However, Bywater and Sharples (2012) claim that the programme on its own is not enough for children to succeed. They suggest that implementing the programme consistently and with additional resources takes time.

Similarly, Rones and Hoagward (2000; cited in Hallam, 2009) agree that SEAL, for example, on its own is not effective. Factors such as consistent implementation of the programme, and input from parents/carers, staff and peers alongside the integration of SEAL into the daily curriculum will help to make it more effective.

In addition to the various pedagogical approaches and intervention programmes discussed thus far, the Welsh Government (2013) and Estyn (2012) claim that parental involvement and strong home–school partnerships in their child's education positively impact on a child's well-being, which subsequently impacts on their learning and life chances. Furthermore, it is reported that when schools provide more activities that are creative and exciting in nature this results in positive child well-being (Estyn, 2013). In addition Estyn (2014), the Education and Training Inspectorate in Wales, state that when the building is poorly maintained, this can have a negative impact on a child's well-being. However, there is often limited robust research evidence to support some of these grand claims about what well-being can offer. There is some evidence to suggest that settings are appropriate contexts for developing and promoting children's well-being, but there are very few studies in the UK that have explored well-being in educational contexts.

Assessing well-being

A discussion on assessing well-being is important because since 2008 practitioners in Wales are expected to provide a score between one and six for children's 'Personal and Social Development, Well-being and Cultural Diversity', one of the seven areas of learning in the Foundation Phase. It is beyond the scope of this chapter to discuss the strengths and weaknesses of various tools, therefore Table 5.2 provides some useful information about tools that have been developed to capture the well-being of young children.

Generally, in relation to Early Years practice there are more objective-type measures available which mean the subjective voice of the younger child often gets overlooked. Some subjective tools exist for children under the age of 8 years and they usually adopt a psychological stance, for example, the Pictorial Self-Concept Scale (Fauth and Thompson, 2009). This tool is aimed at early primary school-aged children and involves 50 picture cards where children are asked to rate themselves using the following categories: 'like me', 'sometimes like me', 'not like me'. Another subjective tool aimed at 5-to-7-year-olds has been developed by researchers at the University of Sussex (Banerjee, 2015). This involves a free online socio-emotional questionnaire that captures children's feelings about school and their peers. An adult may need to assist a child in completing the questionnaire, which can be time-consuming. Children under the age of 8 years also completed questionnaires in the Millennium

Table 5.2 Well-being tools for use with young children

Name of tool/measure	Background information	Aims/purpose of the tool/measure	Tool component(s) & type
The Leuven Involvement Scale (LIS)	First developed in 1976* by Professor Ferre Leavers in Belgium. *From 1991 in the UK.	To provide information about the indicators of the quality of the learning process/educational setting. To give practitioners immediate feedback about their work.	Rating scale 1-to-5
Strengths and Difficulties Questionnaire (SDQ)	First developed in 1997 by Robert Goodman (School of Psychiatry) in the UK	To diagnose children who potentially might need mental health support.	Behavioural screening questionnaire tool (several versions available for researchers, clinicians and educationalists) with 25 items
PERIK	First developed in 1999 by two researchers - Mayr and Ulich in Germany	To develop a practical, not too complex, reliable instrument for pre-school teachers enabling them to observe and record well-being systematically.	Six dimensions with six items, scale rating 1-to-6
Observational tool	First developed in 2010 by Rosemary Roberts in the UK	To record information about children's well-being that informs practitioners about children's interests, their companions, and experiences in a structured way. To help practitioners plan more appropriately for individual children.	Three types of coded observation sheets

Cohort Study and in the evaluation of the Foundation Phase in Wales (Taylor et al., 2015). It seems that questionnaires are a common method for capturing children's subjective well-being.

Generally, the majority of subjective well-being tools are aimed at 8-year-olds and above so there is a tendency to adapt tools for use with younger children. An example of this is evident in the Growing Up in Scotland (GUS) study (Parkes et al., 2014). The report identifies that very little is known about the subjective well-being of children under the age of 10. Therefore, for the purpose of the GUS study Parkes et al. (2014) adapted Huebner's multi-dimensional Life Satisfaction Scale for 7-year-olds.

There are various reasons as to why limited tools exist for children under the age of 8 years. For example, elements of subjective well-being such as life evaluation, personal feelings and meaning in life are abstract ideas that young children might find difficult to understand (Wigelsworth et al., 2010). Fauth and Thompson (2009) state that some people adopt the view that young children are not cognitively able to answer questions such as 'who are you?' However, understanding the feelings of others can start to develop in children as young as 9 months where they begin to develop a sense of self-awareness. Also, at around the age of 15 months young children start to recognise themselves in the mirror (Smidt, 2013). Therefore, it could be argued that children from a young age are capable of responding to 'who are you?' questions through using gestures, facial expressions, making meaning through various artefacts – clay, paint, role-play to name but a few. Furthermore, the New Economics Foundation (2009) suggests there is concern about whether young children are able to report honestly and reliably on their inner feelings and this often creates debate. But equally this argument could apply to adults; they may understand abstract concepts but choose not to report honestly. In other words, they may say what they think the listener wants to hear. Mashford-Scott et al. (2012) further suggest that tools are limited because young children are often viewed and constructed as immature, needy, incompetent and lacking insight.

Another reason associated with the challenge of capturing well-being is the various meanings and interpretations attached to the concept of well-being. For example, it can mean 'happiness', 'quality of life', 'life satisfaction', 'contentment' and so on (Ben-Arieh and Frones, 2011). The challenge arises when one domain (type) or one theory is focused upon and ignores the multi-dimensional nature of the concept. Pollard and Lee's (2003) systematic review of well-being found that measures of well-being were not multi-dimensional, and general claims were being made about well-being having only focused on one domain.

Case studies

Case study 1: Rope swing

A small group of children from a Reception class chose to play with the ropes from a den-building kit outside during free-flow access. They threw the ropes over a free-standing play structure in what seemed to be an attempt to create their own swings. Amy seemed to display very high levels of well-being at this point as she confidently set about tying knots to create the swings. Amy (on the right-hand side in Figure 5.1) seemed to have a clear sense of purpose as she tried to secure the knots and she tested them by pulling several times on the rope (see Figure 5.1).

Figure 5.1   Amy on the right-hand side securing the knots

Amy smiled and talked to herself saying 'that's it, over like that' as she persisted with her self-directed task. When the knots failed she smiled and started her task again, displaying a positive and confident disposition. Meanwhile, Sarah attempted to go on one of the rope swings that had been created by Amy. She watched in anticipation as Amy attempted to secure the knots. Sarah smiled and watched Amy test the rope but when it came apart she frowned and said 'I didn't get to swing'. Sarah sat down miserably and turned her back to the other children, but Amy continued to persevere with the knots. When the

Figure 5.2   Sarah on the left-hand side persevering on getting on the swing

swing was complete and Amy tested the ropes for the last time, she called Sarah who then attempted to get on the swing, but the knot failed. 'Oh!' she exclaimed and stamped her foot whilst scowling. She returned to her previous seated position with her back turned, frowning and rubbing her eyes.

Moments later Amy had fixed the rope swing and Sarah returned for the second time to use the swing. She struggled to get on the swing but persevered with a very determined look on her face (see Figure 5.2).

Sarah attempted to get on the swing and demonstrated that she was both determined and persistent. Once on the swing she showed signs of satisfaction and delight. However, within seconds the swing failed and Sarah fell to the ground. She then walked away from the ropes and sat down on her own and began to cry. The other children seemed absorbed in their task but when the adult said: 'Something has happened to Sarah. Can you check she's OK?' they quickly went over to her and crouched down next to her. 'She's crying coz it keeps breaking' one of the children explained to the adult. Sarah looked at the children and explained that she fell off. She was comforted by her peers and then returned with them to the ropes. Amy tried to make Sarah feel better about herself by pretending to fall off the swing saying that it happened to her too. 'I hurt myself' said Amy. Sarah was willing to have

(Continued)

(Continued)

another go on the swing and she copied the other children by pulling the rope to check it was secure as she persevered with getting herself on the swing. She succeeded with support and encouragement from her peers and seemed extremely happy with the result.

Case study 2: Time to Talk intervention programme

The Time to Talk sessions follow a similar format using a teddy called 'Ginger' and a song about feelings. Jeremy appeared to enjoy the start of the sessions and joined in with the following song:

> 'How do we feel today, how do we feel today?' [Everyone sings]
>
> 'I feel happy today,' sang Jeremy.'
>
> The adult then said: 'That's great Jeremy. Why are you feeling happy today?'
>
> Jeremy replied: 'Because I'm having a picnic with Daddy today.'
>
> 'Oh yes, it's a picnic lunch today. How lovely for you Jeremy,' said the adult.
>
> They then sang the song again and listened to the next child and their feelings.

Figure 5.3   Jeremy and the practitioner working alongside one another

The next part of the group session involved drawing a picture, but Jeremy was unsure how to begin and put his head in his hands.

The adult immediately recognised that Jeremy was a little distressed and reluctant to draw and so reassured him by saying 'It is tricky to know how to start drawing. Let's draw together'. Jeremy appeared to gain confidence through support from a familiar adult and was willing to have a go as they worked alongside each other (see Figure 5.3).

At the end of the group activity Jeremy smiled and laughed as they packed away the resources. He seemed proud of himself and skipped over to show his drawing to another adult in the setting.

Theory into practice

In this section we discuss the two case studies to show how well-being is promoted and supported in the classroom. Case study 1, Rope swing, shows how two children in an EYFS Reception class approach and cope with set-backs during child-initiated play. It also provides examples of the levels within the Leuven Involvement Scale (LIS). The second case study focuses on a Reception-aged child who is involved with a targeted intervention programme called Time to Talk to develop his confidence and general well-being. The programme is designed to develop and enhance oral and social interaction skills for 4-to-6-year-olds (Schroeder, 2001). Both case studies draw upon various theories of well-being identified in Table 5.1 and they demonstrate that well-being is not solely about feelings at a single point in time or how materialistic one feels; it encompasses how human beings interact and communicate with others.

Child-initiated rope swing

Amy seemed deeply engaged with tying knots to create a rope swing and using the Leuven scale to capture levels of well-being from 1 to 5, she could be described as displaying Level 5. This highest level involves a child showing self-confidence, taking pleasure in their activities, being full of energy and self-assured (Laevers et al., 1997). Amy seemed to have a clear sense of purpose as she tried to secure the knots and smiled and talked to herself, which is often an indicator of a higher level on the Leuven scale. Two different philosophical perspectives of well-being are evident in this case study, such as the hedonic/mental states perspective, which is characterised by feelings of happiness and pleasure (Raghavan and Alexandrova, 2015) as well as the eudaimonic/flourishing perspective which encompasses ideas of human functioning and development, autonomy, self-realisation and fulfilment, having a sense of purpose, and fulfilling your potential (Dodge et al., 2012; Thompson and Marks, 2006).

In contrast to Amy, Sarah's efforts to use the rope swing resulted in Level 1 on the Leuven scale. For example, Sarah seemed dejected and angry and withdrew herself from the situation when she failed to succeed. Level 1 on the Leuven scale is described as being in discomfort, withdrawing themselves and being angry (Laevers et al., 1997), which exemplifies the psychological perspective of well-being and 'negative' emotions (McLellan and Steward, 2015). However, Sarah also persevered with the task at hand and once on the swing she showed signs of satisfaction and delight and at that moment she scored Level 4 on the Leuven scale, which includes many of the same indicators as Level 5, but they are not as consistent and intense (Laevers et al., 1997). However, within seconds the swing failed and Sarah fell to the ground but Amy stepped in to help her. At this moment during their play, Amy shows empathy towards Sarah's emotional well-being and highlights the importance of peer relationships (Dowling, 2014). Roberts (2010) suggests that well-being constitutes four main themes and Amy demonstrated all four, such as:

[1] Physical development – when Amy ties the knots and makes a swing
[2] Communication – with Sarah, about making her feel better
[3] Belonging and Boundaries – in her sense of purpose and engagement
[4] Agency – in her persistence to make a fully working swing

Various well-being domains are evident during this case study, such as 'emotional', 'psychological', 'physical' and 'social' well-being, which are commonly associated with young children (Statham and Chase, 2010).

The way in which Sarah engaged in the rope swing shows how well-being fluctuates and how she experiences a range of emotions, which is important for healthy development. Dowling (2014) states that for children to be able to understand their emotions they need to experience a range of them. Watson et al. (2012) and Craig (2009) argue that for children to develop resilience and persistence and to feel motivated to succeed they need setbacks and they need to experience negative emotions.

Seligman (2011; cited in Dodge et al., 2012), who has contributed significantly to developing the positive psychology movement, suggests that well-being constitutes the five constructs he calls PERMA: Positive emotion, Engagement, Relationships, Meaning and Accomplishment. He proposes that well-being is a combination of hedonic and eudaimonic perspectives (McLellan and Steward, 2015). PERMA was demonstrated by Sarah and Amy but in different ways: for example, in the way they showed positive emotions about different achievements.

Time to Talk programme

A Reception-aged child called Jeremy was selected to work with a small group of children to develop his confidence and general well-being by following the Time to Talk targeted programme. The small group situation allows the children to have specific time to talk with an adult or their peers without disruption. This case study is an example of a discrete delivery for well-being as opposed to the integrated delivery.

When Jeremy put his head in his hands this demonstrates two domains suggested by Statham and Chase (2010), namely 'emotional' and 'beliefs' domains. This case study provides an example of the intrapersonal dimension of well-being which focuses more on Jeremy's internalised self, whereas the first case study focused more upon the interpersonal dimension which centres on someone's social circumstances and relationships with others (Fraillon, 2004).

Jeremy is on a journey throughout the session and the outcome of the session resulted in associations with philosophical perspectives of well-being, such as a hedonic/mental states perspective of happiness and pleasure, and a eudaimonic/flourishing perspective where Jeremy felt a sense of achievement and fulfilment. In addition, this case study links with the psychological perspective and 'positive' emotions.

The role of the adult

Both case studies highlight the importance of meaningful, positive relationships between children themselves and between adults and children in promoting and supporting well-being. The OECD (2011) highlight that the quality of a child's relationship with practitioners and a parent/carer is the main contributor to a child's well-being. The case studies also demonstrate the importance of a needs-based philosophical perspective of well-being. This means that adults believe in numerous underlying conditions and prerequisites (Thompson and Marks, 2006)

(Continued)

(Continued)

for well-being to emerge. For example, the prerequisites in Case study 1 included free-flow access and child-initiated play, whereas the prerequisites in Case study 2 included a targeted programme and a supportive and understanding practitioner. Another example of a prerequisite is presented in one of the three prime areas of the Early Years Foundation Stage in England, called 'Personal, Social and Emotional Development', where it states this area is crucial for helping children develop curiosity and enthusiasm in their learning (DfE, 2014).

In the first case study, the children were encouraged to initiate and plan their own play and the duration of the play was not controlled by the adult. Therefore, it could be argued that the children were respected to make their own decisions and the adults appreciated a child's right to play. In turn this leads to positive well-being and self-worth, but more empirical studies are required to strengthen this claim. This first case study reinforces the important message about providing opportunities for children to initiate their own play and for the adult to stand back and observe how children interact with their peers. It also allowed children to experience a range of emotions, and helping children manage their own feelings is a requirement in the Personal, Social and Emotional prime area of the Early Years Foundation Stage in England (DfE, 2014).

When Jeremy, in Case study 2, put his head in his hands and did not know what to draw, the adult encouraged him by drawing a picture and sat beside him. The adult was understanding and appeared to be in tune with his needs. The longitudinal Effective Provision of Pre-school Education (EPPE) study found that when practitioners showed warmth, love and affection as well as responding to their needs the children made substantial progress (Sylva et al., 2004). Laevers (2005) suggests that the personality and temperament of the practitioner are the most important factors that contribute to high levels of well-being in schools, and it is the adult engagement and involvement that has more impact on learning rather than the physical space of the classroom environment or resources used. Laevers (2003) discusses the nature of the practitioners and how this will have the most influence on the child's well-being.

During 2009 to 2011 a project about 'Talking about Young Children's Well-being' took place between London Metropolitan University and the National Children's Bureau. One of the key findings to emerge from this project was the importance of relationships with parents, other close adults and friends for 2-to-6-year-olds (Manning-Morton, 2014). This provides one explanation as to why Jeremy was feeling happy about having a picnic with his father. This also raises the importance of partnership working with children and their families in contributing to child well-being.

Transitions and home–school links

Children will experience various transitions throughout their life stage and well-being will fluctuate. Therefore, it is important for practitioners to be aware of various well-being domains (types) and draw upon the objective and subjective dimensions of well-being in order for them to effectively support and promote well-being. Experiencing transitions allows children to learn to deal with emotions and this can be positively supported by warm, caring, nurturing practitioners.

There is some evidence to suggest that when settings adopt a strong home–school partnership children's well-being is positively influenced and this is mainly reported by inspectorate bodies. Jeremy's response in Case study 2 highlights important people in his life, such as his father, and this should not be underestimated by practitioners. The capabilities approach to understanding well-being which was developed by Sen (1999; cited in Ben-Arieh and Frones, 2011) highlights the importance of recognising children's individual contexts, their interactions and the relationships which influence their well-being. This is a complex interconnected web which practitioners need to acknowledge.

Questions for your practice

[1]   What does well-being mean to you in the context of your practice? Reflect on whether you focus on objective or subjective well-being.
[2]   What well-being domains, also known as types, do you enact/deliver in practice? Are there domains that you favour over others?
[3]   What targeted intervention programmes do you use in practice, and what evidence is there to show they are making improvements to children's well-being?

Summary

This chapter has summarised various well-being perspectives, mainly from the discipline of psychology and philosophy, and highlighted that various domains relate to young children. The two case studies provided useful examples of the various perspectives and domains. They also highlighted the importance of children experiencing and understanding a range of emotions. The role of the adult is important in developing and promoting well-being, particularly, pedagogical practices, such as encouraging child-initiated play and understanding the relevance and importance of children's subjective well-being. Various programmes targeted at improving social and emotional well-being were mentioned, but it was argued that various factors contribute to long-term success rather than just the programme itself. The chapter discussed some tools that practitioners may use to capture children's well-being and the rope swing case study provided examples of the Leuven scale levels. Both case studies demonstrated that well-being fluctuates and consists of interpersonal and intrapersonal aspects and the importance of relationships was also discussed in terms of contributing to children's well-being.

Recommendations for further reading

Collins, J. and Foley, P. (2008) *Promoting Children's Wellbeing: Policy and Practice*. Bristol: The Policy Press. This text provides a useful discussion about promoting children's well-being linked to a range of policy and practice topics, such as children's identity, health and play matters and safeguarding.

Warin, J. (2010) *Stories of Self: Tracking Children's Identity and Wellbeing Through the School Years*. Staffordshire: Trentham Books. This text discusses a longitudinal study of five children as they grow from the age of 3 to 17. It is useful for anyone interested in learning about children's identity.

White, S. and Abeyasekera, A. (2014) *Wellbeing and Quality of Life Assessment: A Practical Guide*. Warwickshire: Practical Action Publishing. This text is structured in four main parts, and part one which is called 'Introduction to wellbeing and quality of life: ideas, issues and choices', provides a good introduction to those wanting to know more about the conceptual nature of well-being.

References

ACCAC (2000) *Desirable Outcome for Children's Learning before Compulsory School Age*. Cardiff: Qualifications, Curriculum & Assessment Authority (ACCAC).

Amerijckx, P. and Humblet, G. (2014) 'Child well-being: What does it mean?', *Children & Society*, 28: 404–15.

Banerjee, R. (2015) [Online] www.sussex.ac.uk/psychology/cress/tools (accessed 13 November 2015).

Bartholomew, R. (2007) *Well-being in the Classroom*. London: The Institute for the Future of the Mind (Transcript of keynote seminar).

Ben-Arieh, A. and Frones, I. (2011) 'Taxonomy for child well-being indicators: A framework for the analysis of the well-being of children', *Childhood*, 18 (4): 460–76.

Bywater, T. and Sharples, J. (2012) 'Effective evidence-based interventions for emotional well-being: Lessons for policy and practice', *Research Papers in Education*, 27 (4): 389–408.

Clack, B. (2012) 'What difference does it make? Philosophical perspectives on the nature of well-being and the role of educational practice, *Research Papers in Education*, 27 (4): 497–512.

Coleman, J. (2009) 'Well-being in schools: Empirical measure, or politicians' dream?', *Oxford Review of Education*, 35 (3): 281–92.

Craig, C. (2009) *Well-being in Schools: The Curious Case of the Tail Wagging the Dog?* Scotland: Centre for Confidence and Well-being.

Davis, E., Priest, N., Davies, B., Sims, M., Harrison, L., Herrman, H., Waters, E., Strazdins, L., Marshall, B. and Cook, K. (2010) 'Promoting children's social and emotional wellbeing in childcare centres within low socioeconomic areas: Strategies, facilitators and challenges', *Australasian Journal of Early Childhood*, 35 (3): 77–86.

DfE (2014) *Statutory Framework for the Early Years Foundation Stage*. London: Department for Education.

Dodge, R., Daly, A., Huyton, J. and Sanders, L. (2012) 'The challenge of defining wellbeing', *International Journal of Wellbeing*, 2 (3): 222–35.

Dowling, M. (2014) *Young Children's Personal, Social and Emotional Development*, 4th edn. London: Sage.

Durlak, J. and Weissberg, R. (2013) *Better evidence-based education – social-emotional learning*. [Online] http://casel.org/wpcontent/uploads/better_social_emotional_learning1.pdf (accessed 18 January 2013).

Ecclestone, K. and Hayes, D. (2009a) *The Dangerous Rise in Therapeutic Education*. Abingdon: Routledge.

Ecclestone, K. and Hayes, D. (2009b) 'Changing the subject: The educational implications of developing emotional well-being', *Oxford Review of Education*, 35 (3): 371–89.

Edwards, S., Skouteris, H., Cutter-Mackenzie, A., Rutherford, L., O'Conner, M., Mantilla, A., Morris, H. and Elliot, S. (2015) 'Young children learning about well-being and environmental education in the early years: A fund of knowledge approach', *Early Years: An International Research Journal*, 30 (1): 1–18.

Ereaut, G. and Whiting, R. (2008) *What Do You Mean by Wellbeing and Why Does It Matter?* London: DCSF.

Estyn (2012) *Effective Practice in Tackling Poverty and Disadvantage in Schools.* Cardiff: Estyn.

Estyn (2013) *Annual Report 2011–2012.* Cardiff: Estyn.

Estyn (2014) *Annual Report 2013–2014.* Cardiff: Estyn.

Fauth, B. and Thompson, M. (2009) *Young Children's Well-Being: Indicators and Domains of Development.* London: National Children's Bureau. Highlight no. 252.

Fraillon, J. (2004) *Measuring Student Well-Being in the Context of Australian Schooling.* Australia: Ministerial Council on Education.

Gasper, D. (2010) 'Understanding the diversity of conceptions of well-being and quality of life', *Journal of Socio-Economics*, 39: 351–60.

Gleave, J. and Cole-Hamilton, I. (2012) *A World Without Play: A Literature Review.* Barnet: Play England.

Hallam, S. (2009) 'An evaluation of the Social and Emotional Aspects of Learning (SEAL) programme: Promoting positive behaviour, effective learning and well-being in primary school children', *Oxford Review of Education*, 35 (3): 313–30.

Humphrey, N., Kalambouka, A., Wigelsworth, M., Lendrum, A., Lennie, C. and Farrell, P. (2010) 'New beginnings: Evaluation of a short social-emotional intervention for primary-aged children', *Educational Psychology*, 30 (5): 513–32.

Laevers, F. (2003) 'Experiential education: Making care and education more effective through well-being and involvement', in F. Laevers and L. Heylen (eds), *Involvement of Children and Teacher Style: Insights from an International Study on Experiential Education.* Leuven: Leuven University Press. pp. 13–24.

Laevers, F. (2005) *Deep-level-learning and the Experiential Approach in Early Childhood and Primary Education.* Research Centre for Early Childhood and Primary Education [Online] http://cego.inform.be/InformCMS/custom/downloads/BO_D&P_Deep-levelLearning.pdf (accessed 2 December 2012).

Laevers, F., Vandenbussche, E., Kog, M. and Depondt, L. (1997) *A Process-oriented Child Monitoring System for Young Children.* Leuven: Centre for Experiential Education.

Manning-Morton, J. (2014) *Exploring Well-being in the Early Years.* Maidenhead: Open University Press.

Mashford-Scott, A., Church, A. and Tayler, C. (2012) 'Seeking children's perspectives on their well-being in early childhood settings', *International Journal of Early Childhood*, 44 (3): 231–47.

Mayr, T. and Ulich, M. (1999) 'Children's well-being in day care centres: An exploratory study', *International Journal of Early Years Education*, 7 (3): 229–39.

McLellan, R. and Steward, S. (2015) 'Measuring children and young people's well-being in the school context', *Cambridge Journal of Education*, 45 (3): 307–32.

New Economics Foundation (2009) *A Guide to Measuring Children's Well-being.* London: New Economics Foundation.

OECD (2006) *Starting Strong II: Early Childhood Education and Care.* London: The Children's Society/OECD Publishing.

OECD (2011) *How's Life? Measuring Well-being.* Paris: OECD Publishing.

Parkes, A., Sweeting, H. and Wright, D. (2014) *Growing Up in Scotland*. Edinburgh: Scottish Government.

Pollard, E. and Lee, P. (2003) 'Child well-being: A systematic review of the literature', *Social Indicators Research*, 61: 59–78.

Raghavan, R. and Alexandrova, A. (2015) 'Toward a theory of child well-being', *Social Indicators Research*, 121: 887–902.

Reber, A. (1995) *Dictionary of Psychology*, 2nd edn. Harmondsworth: Penguin.

Roberts, R. (2010) *Wellbeing from Birth*. London: Sage.

Schroeder, A. (2001) *Time to Talk: A Programme to Develop Oral and Social Interaction Skills for Reception and Key Stage One*. Cambridge: Learning Development Aids.

Seland, M., Sandseter, B. and Bratterud, A. (2015) 'One-to-three-year-old children's experience of subjective wellbeing in day care', *Contemporary Issues in Early Childhood*, 16 (1): 70–83.

Smidt, S. (2013) *The Developing Child in the 21st Century*. Abingdon: Routledge.

Soutter, A., O'Steen, B. and Gilmore, A. (2012) 'Wellbeing in the New Zealand curriculum', *Journal of Curriculum Studies*, 44 (1): 111–42.

Statham, J. and Chase, E. (2010) *Childhood Wellbeing: A Brief Overview*. London: Childhood Wellbeing Research Centre.

Sylva, K., Melhuish, E.C., Sammons, P., Siraj-Blatchford, I., and Taggart, B. (2004) *The Effective Provision of Pre-School Education (EPPE) Project: Technical Paper 12 – the Final Report*. London: DfES.

Taylor, C., Rhys, M., Waldron, S., Davies, R., Power, S., Maynard, T., Moore, L., Blackaby, D. and Plewis, I. (2015) *Evaluating the Foundation Phase: Final Report*. Cardiff: Welsh Government.

Thompson, S. and Marks, N. (2006) *Measuring Well-being in Policy: Issues and Applications*. London: New Economics Foundation.

Waters, J. (2009) 'Well-being', in T. Waller, *An Introduction to Early Childhood*. London: Sage.

Watson, D., Emery, C., Baylis, P., Boushel, M. and McInnes, K. (2012) *Children's Social and Emotional Well-being in School: A Critical Perspective*. Bristol: The Policy Press.

Welsh Government. (2013) *School Effectiveness Framework*. [Online] www.sefcymru.org/sef-p2-home/sef-p2-social_justice/sef-p2-social-justice-engaging-families.htm (accessed 3 January 2013).

Wigelsworth, M., Humphrey, N., Kalambouka, A. and Lendrum, A. (2010) 'A review of key issues in the measurement of children's social and emotional skills', *Educational Psychology in Practice: Theory, Research and Practice in Educational Psychology*, 26 (2): 173–86.

Woolf, A. (2013) 'Social and emotional aspects of learning: Teaching and learning or playing and becoming?', *Pastoral Care in Education*, 31 (1): 28–42.

PLAYING WITH WORDS – BECOMING A READER AND WRITER

Rhiannon Packer, Philippa Watkins and Marc Hughes

Reading this chapter will help you to understand that literacy development is essential as a foundation for all areas of the curriculum. This chapter examines the relationship between speaking, listening, reading and writing, and ways to engage young children in meaningful talk as a precursor for reading and writing. As a consequence it will explore:

- Theories of emergent literacy, the acquisition of literacy by bilingual pupils or those who have English as an Additional Language (EAL) and the role of the practitioner
- The importance of early literacy as a precursor for health and well-being
- The evolving nature of what skills are needed to be literate in the 21st century

---

Key words

emergent literacy, early language acquisition, bilingualism, English as an Additional Language (EAL), digital literacy, home environment, practitioner role

Theoretical perspectives

It is widely accepted that early literacy development is critical for the future health and well-being of children. Children who struggle with literacy in school continue to struggle throughout their adult life. A study carried out by Athanasou (2011) found that literacy levels in childhood were a predictor of education-vocational achievement in adult life. These findings are supported by the OECD (2002), who show low literacy levels have a strongly negative impact upon the broader life course in terms of the inter-generational transmission of poverty and social disadvantage over time.

As such, the critical importance of ensuring successful acquisition of fundamental literacy skills in the early years of childhood cannot be under-estimated. Parents/carers are the first teachers and role models for their children and therefore have a pivotal role in early learning. This needs to be combined with high-quality early learning in settings to ensure that children make the most of their talents and abilities as they develop. Both the Early Years Foundation Stage (EYFS) in England and the Early Years Foundation Phase (EYFP) in Wales emphasise the importance of partner-ship working with parents and/or carers (DfE, 2014; Maynard et al., 2010), making it clear that early learning should be seen a continuum that begins at birth and carries on through the early years and childhood. It becomes of paramount importance, as recognised by the EYFP (WAG, 2008), that what is studied in school builds on each child's prior experi-ence. As a consequence, it is important that Early Years settings work effectively together with parents and/or carers to support young children so that the needs of each child can be met (DCSF, 2008). This makes it clear that successful early literacy learning needs to be progressive.

Brief overview of language acquisition and relation to literacy development

The term 'emergent literacy' was coined in 1966 by Clay in her unpublished doctoral dissertation 'Emergent Reading Behaviour' (University of Auckland, New Zealand). While she originally used the term to describe the stage when children began to receive formal instruction in reading and writing, today it is used to describe the gradual development of language acquisition in children aged from 0 to 4/5 years. The term is used to denote two key ideas in the development of children's early literacy. First, that the early acquisition of language is a process: the term 'emergent' recognises that there are numerous forms of early literacy behaviour. Secondly, 'literacy' reflects the interrelatedness of oracy, reading and writing with a clear understanding that these skills develop concurrently (Sulzby and Teale, 1991).

The development of emergent literacy is complex involving different systems. It should be seen as a developmental continuum in the early life of a child, rather than an absolute phenomenon that begins with formal education (Whitehurst and Lonigan, 1998). It is defined as the concurrent initial development of all aspects of literacy, reading, writing and oral language from early exposure to social contexts in which literacy plays a part (Whitehurst and Lonigan, 1998). That is, emergent literacy develops simultaneously with, and interdependently from, rich exposure to social interaction and environmental stimulus, and in the absence (initially) of formal instruction. In the study of emergent literacy there are several key factors that support successful acquisition. These have been identified as being: the connection between reading and writing; the role of the family in supporting the development of emergent literacy; the value of play as a means of rehearsing and developing skills and understandings; the importance of context and meaning; and the significance of the effective teaching of specific literacy skills (Nutbrown, 1997). This chapter will discuss these factors to enable a comprehensive understanding of how emergent literacy occurs in young children and the importance of effective facilitation by Early Years practitioners.

Initial literacy development begins with the emergence of early communication skills as infants begin to direct others' attention and behaviour (Beuker et al., 2013). Oracy refers to the ability to express through speech, while communication is the conveyance or exchange of information, a necessity for all human beings. During the first few months of life, babies begin to communicate need, such as attention or hunger, by crying, which later develops into babbling at around 5 months. It is at this stage, when the stimulus–response cycle begins, whereby the infant makes a sound and the adult reacts to the sound, encouraging a further response from the infant and thus developing early communication skills (Neaum, 2012). This supports Skinner's behaviourist theory of operant conditioning, which purports that children's verbal language is shaped (Nye, 1979). He suggests that children acquire language through social interaction, that is, children develop oracy by means of reinforcement and imitation (Johnston and Nahamad-Williams, 2009). The importance of providing a language-rich environment for the child in which to develop and enhance linguistic skills is therefore paramount as opportunities are provided that further encourage language use and development. For example, a child babbles 'dadadada' (*stimulus*) and the adult assumes that the child is attempting to say 'daddy' and so provides an encouraging *response*. This positive reinforcement further encourages the child to repeat or imitate the sound and to engage in a communication cycle of making sounds and receiving feedback. In this context the child has a relatively passive role in the process. By reinforcing certain behaviours other people are determining what the child learns (Neaum, 2012). Very often the intonation of repeated utterances by adults to young children is exaggerated, slower, higher-pitched and shorter, with a circling quality to the phrases in comparison with adult-to-adult communication. This is described as 'infant-directed speech' (and has also been referred to as 'motherese') and research has found that young children prefer to listen to talk adjusted in this way (Lindon, 2005).

However, language acquisition goes beyond simply repeating and reinforcing utterances and while the behaviourist theory goes some way in explaining the early acquisition of language, it fails to explain a number of key points. The theory does not provide an explanation of how the volume of language necessary for fluent communication is acquired; nor how children often use words incorrectly which they have not heard before, such as 'go-ed' for 'went'; nor how creative and unique individuals' use of language can be. Providing windows of opportunity in a language-rich environment is paramount for the successful acquisition of language and this begins from birth. If the areas of the brain for language development are not stimulated, then language cannot develop fluently. Children need to actively engage and interact with others to facilitate optimal development, because it is through their encounters with other children and adults that they come across new vocabulary, and are able to construct arguments, express their feelings and develop their fine motor skills (Rushton and Larkin, 2001).

It is fundamental that children are given such opportunities to encourage and facilitate emergent literacy skills. Engagement with the environment and stimulus by others supports the emergence of literacy acquisition. Both the EYFS and the EYFP highlight the significance of the learning environment in supporting and extending children's learning and development. One of the key principles of the EYFS and the EYFP is the importance of creating enabling environments. Through having opportunities to play, both indoors and outdoors, with a balance of child-initiated and adult-led play-based activities, children engage in active learning. This enables them to discover new things, practise ideas and skills, take risks, explore feelings and develop their imagination (DCSF, 2009).

Chomsky questioned the behaviourist approach, arguing from a naturist/ nativist perspective that children are predisposed to learning language, that they are biologically 'prewired' (Ebert, 2005). Research from Kuhl (2004) showed that infants can discriminate among virtually all the phonetic units used in most human languages. However, their initial ability to distinguish between phonetic units does eventually give way to what Kuhl (2004) describes as a language-specific pattern of listening. This means through continued exposure to particular languages they become culturally bound listeners, that is, they focus on the sounds that are familiar to them. Chomsky argues that all individuals are born with an innate ability to acquire the language or languages to which they are exposed and refers to this ability as a 'Language Acquisition Device (LAD)'. Chomsky further developed the concept of a Universal Grammar, surmising that all languages have the same 'grammatical plan' and that this accounts for 'a hypothesized (never demonstrated) acquisitional homogeneity', that is, children acquire language in the same way (Everett, 2016). Chomsky's theory has been challenged from the perspective that there is an over-emphasis on grammar and language structure and little consideration of meaning and social use of language. His theories with regard to language acquisition can be considered rather mechanical as they fail to consider the nuances and uniqueness of creating language. As McBride (2016: 156) points out, the use of language by both parents and children allows them to exchange ideas about the world, the content of which is more important that the grammar. Researchers such as Tomasello (2008) have disputed Chomsky's theory and proposed a usage-based theory of language acquisition, in that children process language through regular use, and this familiarity leads to competence and mastery.

This supports the findings of Vygotsky, who further concentrated upon the social context in which language is learnt. He claimed that it is through dialogue, social interaction and cooperation that understanding can be gained about children's speech and its changes (1984, cited in Daniels, 2005). In Wales, the EYFP not only identifies the importance of speaking and listening within the curriculum (as does the EYFS), but also promotes collaboration and discussion as a key aspect of oracy. Nursery children are expected to participate in discussions with both their peers and others, a skill that is developed through Reception where children are encouraged to exchange their ideas. In Year 1 children contribute to conversations and begin to intentionally use non-verbal cues. By Year 2 they are expected to be able to contribute to discussions and interpret, respond to and use non-verbal cues.

Vygotsky (1978) also developed the concept of the Zone of Proximal Development (ZPD), defined as 'the distance between the actual development level as determined by independent problem-solving and the level of potential development as determined through problem-solving under adult guidance or in collaboration with more capable peer' (p. 86). In the context of emergent literacy, this means that the ZPD can be used to describe the current level of the individual and the potential attainment of the next level with support from adults or peers. Individuals develop literacy competency more effectively when learning, communicating or exploring language with others, especially when those others are more skilled, as it is then they are able to learn and internalise new skills, concepts and psychological tools (Shabani et al., 2010). The role of the Early Years practitioner is to have an understanding of the child's current literacy attainment and to provide appropriate support and guidance to enhance and further develop those skills.

The discourse surrounding language acquisition and the relationship between the neurological function of the brain and its dependence upon social interaction for development highlights the complexity in beginning to understand emergent literacy. Arbib et al. (2014) state that the learning of language is about more than the capacity to interact with the environment but also implicates mechanisms that go beyond a general interaction. This suggests that while a language-rich environment is a vital stimulus for successful language acquisition, humans also have powerful learning mechanisms that make language accessible (Johnston and Nahmad-Williams, 2009). These mechanisms need to be stimulated to work, engaging the brain, as it is experience-expectant and dependent. In this context, Vygotsky's ZPD provides a framework for practitioners to guide further literacy acquisition. His focus was to provide a theoretical basis to support relevant pedagogical interventions, which included principles for grouping learners to enhance their learning, as well as specific interventions for individuals (Shabani et al., 2010).

The concept of an underlying language proficiency and capability for language, and the development of opportunities to practise and apply language in a variety of contexts, has been further developed by Cummins in his concept of the Iceberg theory (1981). Cummins' uses the image of an iceberg to explain his theory of language development and to explain basic interpersonal communicative skills (BICS). Conversational everyday language is developed first, with language used for cognitive and academic proficiency developing later. He proposes a common underlying proficiency (CUP) which allows for the production of language and that this

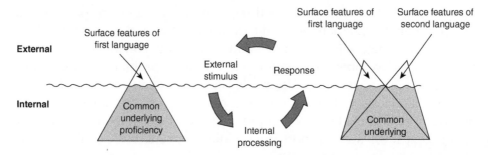

Figure 6.1 Processes of language acquisition and production (based on Cummins' Iceberg model, 1981)

centralised system supports the acquisition of further languages, hence the dual Iceberg model. Figure 6.1 illustrates the importance of developing the CUP to support first language production and further in supporting the acquisition of additional languages.

Children who begin to acquire a second language subsequent to their first language rely on the common underlying proficiency to develop their second language skills. As such it is imperative that these children's first language skills are maintained and developed in order to secure successful second language acquisition and, potentially, bilingualism (Conteh, 2006). The National Association for Language Development in the Curriculum (NALDIC) note that there are over a million bilingual and multilingual children between the ages of 5 and 16 in schools in Britain, between them speaking over 360 different languages, in addition to English (NALDIC, 2016). This does not include children who attend Welsh medium schools and whose first language is English. Evidence from research indicates that EAL learners are likely to underachieve academically compared to their monolingual peers and this attainment gap is of increasing concern (Burgoyne et al., 2011). In addition, research has shown that there is a significant correlation between the home environment and preschool language ability of children regardless of language (Hopkins et al., 2013; Whitehurst and Lonigan, 1998). It is vital, therefore, that preschool and Early Years settings provide opportunities for linguistically rich activities that not only encourage the language of the setting but also opportunities for expressions in the child's home language.

The theories discussed mainly focus on the emergence of language as a whole and do not differentiate as such between the separate language competencies of speaking, listening, reading and writing. Emergent literacy begins with oracy, through speech and hearing, which is typically immediate and unconscious, and occurs as a response to stimulating environments. This is the precursor to the development of literacy that is the ability to make use of the artificial constructs of a symbolic system, which codes information for transmission and retrieval across time and space. As Rushton and Larkin (2001) comment, the emergence of these skills begins with the exploration of letters, sounds and writing which simultaneously increase the ability to interpret, recognise and understand these symbols. In this context, exposure to stimulus is necessary rather than explicit teaching. It is important to recognise that the environment that helps to develop literacy skills in the 21st century is becoming increasingly dominated by the digital world. The multimodality of literacy, that is the flexibility and immediacy in which language is presented, communicated and received in an ever-evolving digital age, means that even before they come into contact with formal education, many young children are already immersed in interactive digital environments (Hopkins et al., 2013). Through these interactions they develop important skills to do with information navigation. They learn to retrieve, decode, decipher, transmit and create information in a variety of formats in a networked and interlinked way. This is long before they are able to read and write on a static page (Hopkins et al., 2013).

The impact of digital technology on the early years is on-going and often underestimated. Flewitt et al. (2015) state that research evidence has consistently shown ambivalence and often a resistance to using digital technologies in early literacy education. However, according to Ofcom (2015), there is evidence of young children having increasing access to tablets that are able to host apps, with recent findings showing that over half of 3–4-year-olds (53%) and 75% of 5–15-year-olds are using tablets. It is possible to argue, then, that if children get most of their education in real life (Vygotsky, 1997) it will be these digital technologies that shape their learning. If young children are growing up as 'digital natives' in a new type of learning environment, then this would suggest that settings will need to supplement their traditional focus on understanding basic concepts about print with an understanding of the digital world. Specific skills are needed to navigate this world, including the ability to understand and use networked information, navigate through linked rather than sequential pages, and interpret visual, aural and verbal information all at the same time (Hopkins et al., 2013).

What is clear is that the emergence of literacy in a child does not occur in isolation, it is rather a synthesis of skills that enables the child to begin to interact and make sense of the surrounding environment.

The following case studies illustrate some of the disparities that exist within settings and highlight some of the barriers faced in terms of good practice as well as demonstrating literacy development in pupils.

Case studies

Case study 1: Mae hi wedi torri ei choes

The setting is a Welsh medium non-maintained nursery school in a relatively affluent semi-urban town in South-East Wales. A maximum of 20 children may attend a morning session from 9.15 to 11.45 am. Welsh is the language of the nursery school, although the majority of children come from English-speaking backgrounds and for many this is their first exposure to the language. Children attend the nursery from the age of 2 years and leave in the term of their fourth birthday to attend the local Welsh medium primary school in the town. All sessions follow the same routine. The children are greeted by name in Welsh at the door by the nursery leader and two practitioners who take their coats and bags, leaving the children free to explore the different play 'zones' that have been set up for them around the nursery. These typically include a reading corner, a kitchen, a climbing frame, sand tray with objects (e.g. dinosaurs), counting blocks and shape-sorting activities on a table. The children are free to play with whatever they choose and with the practitioners overseeing and supporting where necessary, such as encouraging language use when using the counting blocks (identifying number and colour).

At 10.15 the children are told to sit on the mat and, with encouragement from the nursery leader, begin to sing a song while two children at a time go and wash their hands. The song is familiar and the instructions given to the children are repeated time and time again. The children then go to sit at the table, singing another song. The nursery leader then speaks to the group asking questions, such as 'What day is it?', 'How many are here today?' (referring to the number that has been put on the door). They are then given plates (and asked to identify the colour) and have a snack and a drink. The children leave the table one by one having responded to a question posed by the nursery leader. While the children are eating the mid-morning snack, the play activities have been replaced with new ones such as a drawing table, a music corner, a toy pirate ship, a seesaw and jigsaws. The children again have free choice to play and can move from one activity to another. At 11.30 the children sit in a row on chairs and begin to sing songs about the body, using movement to illustrate the songs.

Throughout the session the children are encouraged to speak in Welsh but if they use an English word the practitioner repeats the word back to them in Welsh. For example, a child noticed that another child had broken her leg and drew the attention of the practitioner to the plaster and then to her own leg. The practitioner said to the child, 'Mae hi wedi torri ei choes, she's broken it. Dwyt ti ddim wedi torri dy goes di, rwyt ti wedi'i brifo hi, you've hurt your leg' (Translation: She's broken her leg, she's broken it. You haven't broken your leg, you've hurt it, you've hurt your leg).

At the end of the session, the nursery leader then closes with a final 'goodbye' song and opens the nursery door to parents. Each child is given his/her bag and coat and on the nursery leader's call leaves the session with their parent/guardian. Oral feedback on the child's performance or behaviour during the session is given to the parent/guardian and a written report on overall attainment is provided prior to the child's transition to primary school. Visits to the local feeder school occur during the final term so that the children can familiarise themselves with the new setting.

Case study 2: Developing home–school links

The setting is a two-form-entry primary school in a deprived area of a city in South-East Wales. Approximately 56% of pupils are entitled to Free School Meals (FSM). The school has a nursery and Flying Start setting on site. The majority of children come from English-speaking backgrounds with approximately 9% of pupils coming from homes where English is an Additional Language. Many pupils enter Flying Start or the nursery setting with very low baseline scores in social, literacy and numeracy skills.

Breakfast Club is available to all children from 8 am, which 10–15% of the pupils attend. Most pupils who attend Breakfast Club do not eat in the morning before attending. There are also some pupils who do not attend Breakfast Club and often do not have breakfast at home before coming to school at 9 am.

Many of the pupils who attend Flying Start on the school site move onto the nursery setting at the school. The school works closely with Flying Start with regular monthly meetings between the head teacher and the lead practitioner from the Flying Start setting. There are also regular informal discussions between the nursery teacher and Flying Start staff as well as structured termly meetings. These meetings

(Continued)

(Continued)

provide an opportunity to discuss all the pupils from Flying Start and their academic and social development. What is very apparent from these meetings is that many of the pupils are already functioning at a very low literacy level when they first attend the Flying Start setting. Some of the pupils have very limited speaking and listening skills.

Developing home–school links has been a focus for the school. There is a Family Champion member of staff who works for 22 hours a week with a sole focus on parental engagement. Various strategies are used to improve home–school links and the literacy skills of pupils and parents. These include 'lads and dads' reading days, home/school reading schemes and many other activities, including fundraising events. This has been successful with a core number of families and has shown positive outcomes for literacy skills over time. However, it is evident that the same few families are engaging each time. Statistically very few families of SEN pupils or those with initial lower literacy skills have engaged with the school's Family Champion. These pupils have been prioritised many times in an attempt to raise the basic literacy skills of pupils and parents. Unfortunately, there remains a reluctance in a majority of families to engage in any initiative. After discussions with some of the prioritised families it was discovered that they had a negative attitude towards education and its value. This highlights current issues in developing and enhancing family, community and educational engagement.

Theory into practice

The theoretical perspectives outlined in the overview espouse the vital importance of the child's environment, in particular, the home, in supporting emergent literacy. McBride (2016) identifies a number of environmental influences that affect language development, which include the language spoken at home, home environment and socio-economic status, and classroom teaching style. Early Years practitioners can only directly impact upon the latter, so an understanding of the theories surrounding language development and emergent literacy is imperative for effective practice in the preschool and Early Years setting. The role of the practitioner is to reinforce the learning that has already taken place, and to provide contexts for learning through scaffolding. In a school week children in full-time education spend under 20% of their time in the setting. While the role of the practitioner is critical, it is evident that the home environment has a huge impact upon emergent literacy. This section will discuss how the connections between theories regarding language acquisition and emergent literacy link with practice, illustrated using examples from the case studies.

Hopkins et al. (2013: 26) state that before children can become literate through formal education, they already need to have developed the cognitive, non-cognitive and social skills on which learning depends. This includes the ability to self-regulate. The home environment is critical, therefore, in ensuring the linguistic, cognitive and social preparation of the child before starting school. However, when the home environment is unable to, or does not, provide the appropriate skills necessary for literacy acquisition, then preschool and Early Years settings play a fundamental role, especially if the link between deprivation and poor educational attainment is to be broken (Welsh Government, 2014). Hopkins et al. (2013) further comment that exposure to high-quality early childhood education has a positive effect on children's learning, language and cognitive development. This is particularly true of the children who have the greatest need, both economically and socially.

The quality of education described does not necessitate formal teaching but rather planned opportunities for the burgeoning of social skills. It also includes understanding the contextual role and use of language and developing a set of competencies and skills, thus enabling the journey of a dependent child transforming into an independent adult. Critical to this transformation is the strength of the foundation of emergent literacy in the individual, and the Early Years practitioner can play a pivotal role in narrowing any potential disparities. As Jones (2012) states, intentional strategies to promote oracy can improve literacies between students from economically and socially deprived backgrounds. Recognising the importance of early language acquisition from research has resulted in a number of government support schemes such as Flying Start, Pori drwy Stori and Bookstart, with the purpose of educating parents in socially deprived areas on the importance of communication with their children (Welsh Government, 2014). Governmental policies and documentation, such as *Rewriting the Future: Raising Ambition and Attainment in Welsh schools* (Welsh Government, 2014) and *Building a Brighter Future: Early Years and Childcare Plan* (Welsh Government, 2013a), are guided by research and theories for implementation into practice. The identification that it is imperative that preschool and Early Years settings enable children to access universal, high-quality education evidences the intention to mitigate any potential discrepancies, so that learners are ready to begin formal schooling and early language skills are well developed. However, even with excellent practice, positive parental involvement and engagement are crucial in order for the child to reach their full potential, as evidenced in Case study 2 where parents are reluctant to become involved in any home–school initiatives.

The impact of a high-quality education has been evidenced through the discussion but understanding how to implement and ensure quality of delivery requires further explanation. Three key aspects will be presented which provide a platform for preschool and Early Years practitioners to develop effective emergent literacy acquisition in the child, namely, providing stimulating and safe environments for learning; ensuring that settings are responsive to need; and engaging with families to further support and enhance learning. The aspects considered are evaluated from an emergent literacy perspective, but have the potential to encompass other facets of a child's holistic development.

Children need to feel safe and secure in their environment before they can be responsive to new experiences and stimuli (Rushton and Larkin, 2001). Ensuring that basic needs are met (in line with Maslow's Hierarchy of Needs (1970) and supported by Brazelton and Greenspan's (2000) irreducible needs of children) is essential if there is to be effective higher cognitive functioning. For example, before children can be motivated to process, engage and understand new ideas and concepts their physiological requirements (i.e. food and drink) need to be satisfied. A practical application to address one aspect is free breakfast clubs (as seen in Case study 2) for all children in schools across Wales.

The Early Years environment needs to be constant and familiar, providing a sense of connection and ownership on behalf of the child so that language development can be reinforced and enhanced, as evidenced in Case study 1. Conteh (2006) suggests that this can be achieved through collaborative talk where classroom discussion allows for children to contextualise their learning within concrete experiences, enabling scaffolding to occur as children move from concrete to abstract activity, thinking and using language, which also provides opportunities for revisiting and using language. Opportunities for collaborative talk can occur during first-hand experiential situations, such as when playing with peers, and in circle time sessions, small group discussion and whole class deliberations, allowing children to learn from others and to explore, practise and develop new language skills. This is evidenced in Case study 1, where the nursery leader asks the children questions during snack time and other children are encouraged to participate in the discussion and to reiterate new words that have been introduced into the conversation.

Taking ownership of the environment, feeling an integral part of the setting and reinforcing language can be achieved by using language visually around the setting and maintaining familiar routines. Labelling key items around the classroom and making reference where necessary, providing opportunities to mark-make and to discuss, are examples of encouraging links between reading and oracy and provide a further connection of ownership in the Early Years environment. This is evidenced in Case study 1, where the children verbally count how many are in the class and the nursery leader refers them to a visual image of the number on the wall. The sessions in the nursery follow a consistent routine and the use of songs to denote the end of a session or the beginning of another reinforces language use within a structured and safe environment. During snack time children are asked questions about body parts in Welsh, e.g. *Ble mae dy drwyn?* (Where is your nose?), which connect with the songs that are sung during the sessions. Language development in this context is meaningful and has purpose, allowing for children to explore their own understanding in new contexts.

Activities in settings need to be carefully organised to ensure that they are linguistically appropriate and achievable through support (scaffolding) while also providing stimulus. The challenge is to ensure that the stimulus is sufficient to engage but not too demanding in that completion of the task is unachievable and demoralising. As Rushton and Larkin (2001) comment, differentiation of activities allows all children to take part and gives them access to content, ideas and conversation with their peers. The Foundation Phase and the Early Years Foundation Stage provide guidance on what is appropriate and achievable at the different stages of language development, separating it into three strands – oracy, reading, writing – and identify the appropriate knowledge and understanding expected at each stage (Welsh Government, 2015). Alongside the Foundation Phase, the National Literacy and Numeracy Framework (LNF) (Welsh Government, 2012) supports practitioners in embedding literacy and numeracy in all aspects of the curriculum from age 3. Guidance is given to practitioners with regard to the type of language skills that should be evidenced and activities that support relevant language skills development. Practitioners need to create a responsive environment, identifying and addressing need appropriately. For example, in a bilingual setting, such as in Case study 1, while the language of the setting is Welsh, children are able to express themselves in English and the practitioner responds accordingly, using Welsh first and then ensuring understanding, if necessary, with English. This supports Cummins' dual Iceberg theory while also connecting with the 'Oracy across the curriculum' strand of the LNF as the children are communicating clearly with others.

Research by Adams (1990) estimated that the typical child from a middle-class background begins formal schooling with between 1,000 and 1,700 hours of one-on-one picture book reading in comparison with a child from a more deprived background, who on average has just 25 hours. Such a discrepancy in quality contact time significantly impacts upon the development of a child's emergent language skills, as before the age of 2 it is estimated that a child's receptive vocabulary is four times greater than their speaking vocabulary (Ard and Beverly, 2004). Sticht (2012) also notes that there is a difference of 153,000 in the number of words between what a child from a deprived background hears per week (62,000 words on average) and a child from an advantaged home hears (215,000 words). In addition, research has found that extratextual talk, that is discussion surrounding the book which is being read, has a greater impact upon vocabulary development in preschool children (Blewitt and Langan, 2016). Focusing on specific types of extratextual talk has proven to further increase word learning, such as asking children questions about vocabulary, defining and explaining, and providing synonyms for new words (Blewitt and Langan, 2016). Providing opportunities for children to develop good reading habits is fundamental to successful literacy, and so providing opportunities for reading in preschool settings such as the 'lads and dads' reading days and the home–school reading scheme sessions in Case study 2 is vital. It is interesting to note that one of the most dominant influences today, the prevalence of the digital world, is not evident in either of the case studies.

Transitions and home–school links

In terms of academic transition – especially to do with early oracy – development in Wales is guided by the structure of the LNF. The LNF is designed to be a curriculum planning tool which supports all teachers (Welsh Government, 2013b). It focuses on learners' acquisition of and ability to apply the skills and concepts appropriate to their stage of development, and it traces these expectations from the Routes for Learning route map (Department for Education, Lifelong Learning and Skills, 2006), into the Routes for Literacy and Numeracy, into the Foundation Phase and then into Key Stages 2, 3 and 4. Skills are therefore developed on a continuum, with progression through oracy, reading and writing clearly identified. It is this structure that helps provide a secure framework as children transition through the education system.

Engaging and involving parents is crucial in the holistic literacy development of the child. It is suggested that parental involvement with educational settings significantly improves academic performance (Welsh Government, 2014). Encouraging parental involvement in educational settings is a challenge, as noted in Case study 2, where those children in greatest need of home literacy support very often are reluctant to engage due to the parents' own educational values, experiences and attitudes. Evidence from a report by the Joseph Rowntree Foundation (2013) identified that parents with poor literacy skills were far more likely to be apathetic about the importance of modelling reading at home and to see school as the sole focus of learning. Engaging such marginalised groups of parents is a constant challenge in the effort to break the negative literacy cycle. While acknowledging the contribution home environment makes in supporting emergent literacy, increasing the involvement of disengaged families is a constant challenge for practitioners and policy-makers alike (Welsh Government, 2014).

In the constant drive to improve educational standards in Wales, the government has identified the necessity to improve literacy standards across the educational system. To do this it is vitally important that practitioners in the Early Years recognise the value of emergent literacy and the multi-faceted way in which is it acquired. Preparing preschool and Early Years settings to provide a safe and constant environment for learning, to be responsive to the individual needs of learners and to encourage the engagement of parents in their child's learning in order to optimise opportunities for the development of emergent literacies is a challenge. The case studies demonstrate that practitioners create learning environments which encourage language-rich opportunities and are responsive to individual need.

Questions for your practice

[1] How do you use language in your setting and model it for children?
[2] How can you encourage good reading habits in your setting?
[3] In what ways can you encourage families to engage in developing their children's literacy?

Summary

This chapter has identified the importance of the early development of language and literacy in children. It has highlighted the critical role of the home environment in developing these skills and identifies challenges faced by practitioners where support is lacking. Settings need to employ strategies that not only motivate pupils but engage parents as well. To do this, it is imperative that relationships between parents and schools are positive and that the support offered is responsive to need. Practitioners need to ensure that settings provide language rich supportive environments that encourage children to play, respond and develop language skills.

Recommendations for further reading

Conteh, J. (ed.) (2006) *Promoting Learning for Bilingual Pupils 3–11. Opening Doors to Success*. London: Sage. Detailed information about educating bilingual/EAL learners and how to promote effective learning. Practical advice given as well as explanations of theories with regards to bilingualism.

McBride, C. (2016) *Children's Literacy Development: A Cross-Cultural Perspective on Learning to Read and Write*. London: Routledge. This text provides an understanding of the complexities in literacy development from a cross-cultural perspective.

Johnston, J. and Nahmad-Williams, L. (2009) *Early Childhood Studies*. London: Pearson Education. A very good guide to support practitioners in placement. Provides opportunity for reflective thinking.

References

Adams, M. J. (1990) *Beginning to Read: Thinking and Learning about Print*. Cambridge, MA: MIT Press.

Arbib, M. A., Gasser, B. and Barrès, V. (2014) 'Language is handy but is it embodied?' *Neuropsychologia*, 55: 57–70.

Ard, L. M. and Beverly, B. L. (2004) 'Preschool word learning during joint book reading: effect of adult questions and comments', *Communication Disorders Quarterly*, 26 (1): 17–28.

Athanasou, J. (2011) 'Is adult reading a guide to educational-vocational achieve-ment?' *Australian Journal of Career Development*, 20 (2): 15.

Beuker, K. T., Rommelse, N. N. J., Donders, R. and Buitelaar, J. K. (2013) 'Development of early communication skills in the first two years of life', *Infant Behavior and Development*, 36: 71–83.

Blewitt, P. and Langan, R. (2016) 'Learning words during shared book reading: The role of extratextual talk designed to increase child engagement', *Journal of Experimental Child Psychology*, 150: 404–40.

Brazelton, T. and Greenspan, S. (2000) *The Irreducible Needs of Children: What Every Child Must Have to Grow, Learn and Flourish*. Cambridge, MA: Da Capo Press.

Burgoyne, K., Whiteley, H. E. and Hutchinson, J. M. (2011) 'The development of comprehension and reading-related skills in children learning English as an additional language and their monolingual, English speaking peers', *British Journal of Psychology*, 81: 344–54.

Clay, M. (1966) 'Emergent reading behaviour' (Unpublished doctoral dissertation). University of Auckland, New Zealand.

Conteh, J. (ed.) (2006) *Promoting Learning for Bilingual Pupils 3–11*. London: Sage.

Cummins, J. (1981) *Bilingualism and Minority Language Children*. Toronto: Ontario Institute for Studies in Education.

Cummins, J. (2011) 'Literacy engagement: Fueling academic growth for English learners', *Reading Teacher*, 65 (2): 142–6.

Daniels, H. (2005) *An Introduction to Vygotsky*. London: Routledge Ebook (accessed 5 August 2016).

DCSF (Department for Children, Schools and Families) (2008) *Practice Guidance for the Early Years Foundation Stage*. Available at: http://www.foundationyears.org.uk/wp-content/uploads/2011/10/EYFS_Practice_Guide1.pdf (accessed 2 November 2016).

DCSF (Department for Children, Schools and Families) (2009) *Learning, Playing and Interacting: Good Practice in the Early Years Foundation Stage*. Available at: www.foundationyears.org.uk/wp-content/uploads/2011/10/Learning_Playing_Interacting.pdf (accessed on 2 November 2016).

DfE (Department for Education) (2014) *Statutory Framework for the Early Years Foundation Stage: Setting the standards for learning, development and care for children from birth to five*. Available at: www.gov.uk/government/uploads/system/uploads/attachment_data/file/335504/EYFS_framework_from_1_September_2014__with_clarification_note.pdf (accessed 2 November 2016).

Department for Education, Lifelong Learning and Skills (2006) *Routes for Learning*. Cardiff: Crown.

Ebert, J. (2005) 'Tongue-tied', *Nature*, 438 (7065): 148–9.

Everett, D. L. (2016) 'An evaluation of universal grammar and the phonological mind', *Frontiers in Psychology*, 7: 15. Published online 8 February 2016 doi: 10.3389/fpsyg.2016.00015 (accessed 8 August 2016).

Flewitt, R., Messer, D. and Kucirkova, N. (2015) 'New directions for early lit-eracy in a digital age: The iPad', *Journal of Early Childhood Literacy*, 15 (3): 289–310.

Hopkins, L., Brookes, F. and Green, F. (2013) 'Books, bytes and brains: The implications of new knowledge for children's early literacy learning', *Australasian Journal of Early Childhood*, 38 (1).

Johnston, J. and Nahmad-Williams, L. (2009) *Early Childhood Studies*. London: Pearson Education.

Jones, N. A. (2012) 'Preschool educators' perceptions of practice in facilitating/modeling oral language acquisition and development', *Dissertations*. Paper 356. http://ecommons.luc.edu/luc_diss/356and Development (accessed 11 August 2016).

Joseph Rowntree Foundation (2013) *Poverty and Ethnicity in Wales*. York: Joseph Rowntree Foundation.

Kuhl, P. (2004) 'Early language acquisition: Cracking the speech code', *Nature Reviews: Neuroscience*, 5: 831–43.

Lindon, J. (2005) *Understanding Child Development: 0–8 Years*. London: Hodder Arnold.

Maslow, A. (1970) *Motivation and Personality*, 2nd edn. New York: Harper & Row.

Maynard, T., Morgan, A., Waters, J. and Williams, J. (2010) *The Teaching and Learning Research Programme in Wales: The Foundation Phase*. Available at: http://dera.ioe.ac.uk/1866/1/101202foundationreporten.pdf (accessed 2 November 2016).

McBride, C. (2016) *Children's Literacy Development: A Cross-cultural Perspective on Learning to Read and Write*. London: Routledge.

NALDIC (2016) EAL statistics: The latest EAL facts and figures. www.naldic.org.uk/research-and-information/eal-statistics/ (accessed 9 August 2016).

Neaum, S. (2012) *Language and Literacy for the Early Years*. London: Sage.

Nutbrown, C. (1997) *Recognising Early Literacy Development*. London: Paul Chapman Publishing.

Nye, R. D. (1979) *What is B.F. Skinner Really Saying?* London: Prentice–Hall.

OECD (2002) *Reading for Change: Performance and Engagement across Countries. Executive Summary*. Paris: OECD.

Ofcom (2015) *Children and Parents: Media Use and Attitudes Report*. [Online] Available at: http://oro.open.ac.uk/40612/1/New%20directions%20for%20early%20literacy%20in%20a%20digital%20age%20AAM.pdf (accessed 14 June 2016).

Rushton, S. and Larkin, E. (2001) 'Shaping the learning environment: Connecting developmentally appropriate practices to brain research', *Early Childhood Education Journal*, 29 (1).

Shabani, K., Khatib, M. and Ebadi, S. (2010) 'Vygotsky's Zone of Proximal Development: Instructional implications and teachers' professional development', *English Language Teaching*, 3 (4). [Online] doi: http://dx.doi.org/10.5539/elt.v3n4p237 (accessed 9 August 2016).

Sticht, T. (2012) 'Getting it right from the start: The case for early parenthood education', *American Educator*. www.aft.org/sites/default/files/periodicals/Sticht.pdf (accessed 16 August 2016).

Sulzby, E. and Teale, W. (1991) 'Emergent literacy', in R. Barr, B. Kamil, P. Mosenthal and P. Pearson (eds), *Handbook of Reading Research*, Vol. 2. New York: Longman. pp. 727–58.

Tomasello, M. (2008) *The Usage-based Theory of Language Acquisition*. [Online] Available at: www.princeton.edu/~adele/LIN_106:_UCB.../ BavinChapter09.pdf (accessed 4 August 2016).

Vygotsky, L. S. (1978) *Mind in Society: The Development of Higher Psychological Processes*. Cambridge, MA: Harvard University Press.

Vygotsky, L. S. (1997) *Educational Psychology*. Boca Raton, FL: CRC Press.

WAG (Welsh Assembly Government) (2008) *Learning and Teaching Pedagogy*. Available at: www.wales.gov.uk (accessed on 2 November 2016).

Welsh Government (2012) *National Literacy and Numeracy Framework*. Cardiff: Welsh Government.

Welsh Government (2013a) *Building a Brighter Future: Early Years and Childcare Plan*. Cardiff: Welsh Government.

Welsh Government (2013b) *Curriculum Planning Guidance*. Cardiff: Welsh Government

Welsh Government (2014) *Rewriting the Future: Raising Ambition and Attainment in Welsh Schools*. Cardiff: Welsh Government.

Welsh Government (2015) *Curriculum for Wales: Foundation Phase Framework (Revised 2015)*. Cardiff: Welsh Government.

Whitehurst, G. J. and Lonigan, C. J. (1998) 'Child development and emergent literacy', *Child Development*, 69 (3): 848–72.

DEVELOPING MATHEMATICAL CONFIDENCE IN THE EARLY YEARS

Catherine Jones

Reading this chapter will help you to understand:

- The importance of early intervention to develop mathematical confidence
- The expectations of both the Foundation Phase and Foundation Stage for children's mathematical development
- The joint role that practitioners and parents can play in developing mathematical confidence
- How mathematical concepts and numeracy can be easily incorporated into everyday experiences

Mathematics is often seen as just being about the right answer, but by focusing on this you miss the importance of all the creative processes, thought and problem-solving that should be valued. This chapter is about the importance of the story in mathematical learning not just the final answer.

Mathematics education is under significant scrutiny at all levels of education. The emphasis in the Early Years statutory frameworks in England and Wales is a focus on children interpreting and expressing their everyday experiences in a mathematical way. This is supported by research into effective mathematics teaching that states that analysing real world problems in a mathematical way is an effective way of engaging and being confident with key mathematical processes (Ginsburg, 2009; Treffers and Beishuizen, 1999).

All children are born with the ability to appreciate numbers and as part of their early learning we encourage them to count, sort and recognise patterns and shapes. However the perception of 'I can't do maths' is perpetuated. An OECD Survey of Adult Skills (2013) found that there are an estimated 9 million working-aged adults in England with low literacy or numeracy skills or both. Numeracy skills are well below the average compared to other countries. The first recommendation of the report based on the results of this survey stresses that priority should be given to early intervention to ensure that all young people have stronger basic skills (Kuczera et al., 2016). In England, the 2013–14 Early Years Foundation Stage Profile (EYFSP) data revealed that mathematics and literacy remain the areas of learning with the lowest percentage of children achieving at least the expected level – literacy (61%) and mathematics (66%).

What can we do as Early Years practitioners to ensure that children and parents are confident with numbers and mathematical concepts and the perception of 'I can't do maths' is not perpetuated? This chapter considers what can contribute to a successful learning experience; it looks at the expectations of the Foundation Phase and Foundation Stage, case studies that inform practice, and critically, the role that parents can play in their child's development.

Key words

early intervention, confidence, learning through experience, creativity, learning in partnership, social constructivism

Theoretical perspectives

Children need an engaging and encouraging environment for their early encounters with mathematics to develop their confidence in their ability to understand and use mathematics. Positive experiences support the development of curiosity, imagination, problem-solving and persistence (Clements et al., 2004). Much of the literature and guidance document emphasise the importance of practitioners 'seeing' the mathematics in children's play (DCSF, 2009). This can be realised in three key ways:

- Share positive beliefs about young children learning mathematics
- Be aware of the mathematics that arises through children's self-initiated play
- Have high expectations of young children's mathematical understanding. Children and practitioners should not be frightened and should embrace the subject which is so embedded in much of what we do.

Table 7.1 Overview of mathematical themes for statutory frameworks in Wales and England

Foundation Phase (Wales)	Literacy and Numeracy Framework (Wales)	Foundation Stage (England)
Developing numerical reasoning	Developing numerical reasoning	Using mathematics in real-life situations
Using number skills	Using number skills	Understanding number
Using measuring skills	Using measuring skills	Measures
Using geometry skills		Shape and space
Using data skills	Using data skills	Patterns and relationships

Nunes et al. (2009) differentiate between arithmetic as completing sums and problem-solving and mathematical reasoning as the primary factor that needs to be learnt in order to solve mathematical problems. Both the Foundation Phase in Wales and the Early Years Foundation Stage in England set out expectations for mathematics and numeracy. In Wales, there are particular challenges being focused on: curriculum design, changing perceptions, professional development of both new and current practitioners and ensuring that interventions are timely and appropriate when children are struggling with numeracy. The revised Foundation Phase framework (Welsh Government, 2015) stresses the importance of learning through real-life examples. This concept of 'authentic' learning is being seen as critical throughout the learner's journey from Early Years to higher education level. The revised Early Years Foundation Stage framework (DfE, 2014) emphasises playing, exploring and experiencing. The links to active learning are clear to see as children are encouraged to be resilient if they encounter challenges and, importantly, enjoy achievements.

Although at times using slightly different vocabulary, children in all areas and particularly mathematics should be inspired to create and think critically, develop their own ideas, make links between ideas, and develop strategies for doing things.

Whether it is the Foundation Phase or the Early Years Foundation Stage, the key themes are:

- solving mathematical problems, particularly incorporated into real-life activities, and to make use of their knowledge and understanding of mathematics to solve problems
- communicating mathematically and being given the opportunities to do this orally, pictorially and in writing
- reasoning mathematically and applying those skills across the key areas of learning.

If we look at two key educational theorists as part of this discussion, they strongly support the importance of active learning. Vygotsky (1978) saw mathematics as the development of thinking and reasoning skills and as we will see later in the chapter his idea of a 'Zone of Proximal Development' is very relevant in this context. Vygotsky suggested that concepts are acquired *externally* in discussion or by doing and then at different rates (particularly in the early years) become *internalised* as ways of thought. Piaget (1952) felt that all children are capable of good mathematical reasoning. If learning is personalised and the activity is of interest to the child, this can remove the feelings of insecurity and anxiety that can impede the development of mathematical development. The use of active methods allows the child to explore and experiment on their own terms. The teacher is essentially a facilitator and a creator of learning situations. This fits well with the ethos of the statutory foundation frameworks in England and Wales.

The role of the adult

Teachers have a proactive role to create an environment that supports development at different paces and scaffolding for learning. Essentially what is needed is collaborative/cooperative learning where the co-construction of meaning is based on an awareness and understanding of the child's perspective. The teacher is critical in ensuring that pupils have a safe and supportive environment to develop their mathematical and numeracy skills. It is important to:

- Identify children's current individual knowledge and skills and where they are in relation to statutory frameworks and knowledge about certain 'milestones' or growth points with respect to the mathematics development. This is done with the understanding that in the early years there is variation in development. It is critical to focus on the individual.
- Lead children into their 'Zone of Proximal Development' (Vygotsky, 1978), i.e. the area between a child's level of independent performance (what he/she can do alone) and the child's level of assisted performance (what he/she can do with support).

Case studies

Case study 1: Working with future Early Years practitioners

The first case study focuses on sessions with students on an Early Years course. The students were all final year undergraduate students who been on at least one school placement. The study was done with three cohorts. Groups were asked to reflect on their experiences of mathematics and numeracy in the classroom from both a personal and practitioner perspective and to think about the challenges in delivering mathematics and numeracy and how they could overcome them.

Groups were asked to consider three questions and how they influenced their practice:

- What were your experiences of learning maths?
- Why is maths seen as a difficult subject by some?
- What is the best way to learn maths?

Following the discussion, groups were tasked with designing a mathematical activity. Groups were then given a choice of props to use that may or may not have an obvious mathematical link and were asked to design a mathematics- or numeracy-based activity for either 0–3 years or 3–5 years. Each group was observed as it chose its focus and planned the activity. Common themes in the discussion were that they had not seen the everyday relevance or value of maths as learners themselves and were positive about how the Foundation Phase/Stage was actively promoting this. Maths makes some people feel anxious, leading them to avoid situations where they may have to use mathematics (Chinn, 2012). This was true of many of the students in the group and what they could see in the current Early Years curricula in England and Wales was an emphasis on problem-solving and exploration and not a focus on right and wrong answers. The groups were asked to think about different theorists and pedagogical approaches and which were most effective in teaching mathematics and numeracy. This could then be incorporated into their planning. The outcome of the discussions led to the following definitions. Behaviouralist approaches were about 'mathematics is for knowing'. The value of being able to memorise basic facts was acknowledged but the most support was for the constructivist position of 'mathematics is for understanding' where learning has a scaffold and learning through experience provided a deeper, embedded understanding of mathematics.

A range of props was provided: plastic coloured balls; polystyrene rings; dominoes; wooden marble run (made up of wooden blocks of different colours, shapes and sizes); a book based on a counting game; a jenga-style game with hedgehogs; Dobble (card-matching game); plastic fruit, vegetables, food and large Lego-style bricks. As a group we also discussed how we could use household objects as props. The aim was to see mathematics opportunities in everyday objects and experiences too.

This was a successful example of watching theory being put into practice. The groups were encouraged to look at the props through the eyes of a child and 'play' with the items before deciding the focus of the activity. Important questions were discussed, such as how much instruction should the children be given or would the principles of Montessori methods in mathematics be better and allow the children to explore concepts on their own terms. Observing the students helped the tutor to understand their mathematical understanding and the ways in which their practice could be supported. Also, as in a classroom situation, the practitioner's own interests came into view as they chose the props and concepts they were most confident with.

Each group produced a plan for an activity based on their chosen prop and concepts linked to key milestones in either the Foundation Phase or Foundation Stage. The plan was a mix of purposeful play and adult-led and child-initiated activity. It should support the development of confident mathematicians. The plan had the following headings:

Title: (focus and age ranged aimed at)

Learning Outcomes: (linked to FP/FS outcomes)

Reference to Literacy and Numeracy Framework (Wales): children should be given opportunities to:

Key Skills:

Key Vocabulary: taking away, highest number first, order of size, sort by type, matching

(Continued)

(Continued)

Resources:

Introduction: whole class (10–15 minutes)

Main Activity: (one teacher-led and one independent)

Coming Together: whole class (10–15 minutes)

Additional Activities: activities that could be done at home.

Differentiation:

Feedback: How will you determine whether children have learned what was intended?

The exercise provided a scaffold for practitioners to ensure a balance between child- and teacher-led activities and clear links to statutory frameworks and expected outcomes. The opportunity to be creative with the props worked for the practitioners who, once some got over their initial shyness, used the props in imaginative ways to create mathematics sessions that were not threatening but still built up the skills and vocabulary that are required for expected outcomes in both the Foundation Stage and Foundation Phase. The session also ensured that the groups built into their thinking how learning could be taken into the home environment and had to develop an activity that linked and reinforced the concepts covered.

Case study 2: Using apps to encourage confidence, creativity and partnership learning

At this early stage of a child's development, parents can play a critical role in both development and confidence. Working in partnership with parents is the most effective means of ensuring coherence and continuity in children's experiences, and in the curriculum offered to them. Also, this case study illustrates that everyday experiences are a great source for genuine mathematical problem-solving and practice. One example of successful practice is researching and providing apps for children to use with their parents. Mobile technology can be an excellent way to support children and parents to work together. Calder (2011, 2015) and Calder and Campbell (2016) have carried out extensive work in the value of apps in mathematical learning and stress the role they play in providing alternative ways to facilitate understanding in an active and exploratory way.

There is a growing number of apps that can support learning in a wide range of mathematical concepts. The apps in Table 7.2 were used with a group of 3-to-5-year-olds to observe their interaction, engagement and confidence with the concepts. Different apps are appearing all the time and the following criteria were used to choose the ones in this case study:

- Age-specific mathematics apps that have been positively reviewed
- Educational games (often based on everyday experiences) to practise numeracy and mathematical concepts
- Puzzles that test and develop concepts such as pattern and shape recognition
- Apps that develop knowledge and understanding that can be used in everyday activities.

Children of all ages liked the repetitive nature of many of the tasks and were content to repeat the tasks that as adults we may find boring. This was particularly true with the Toca Store app which was deceptively simple but developed matching and simple money skills. Two of the children devised a way that they could play with this app by taking different shop roles. Maths 3–5 and Maths 4–6 have been trialled by Nottingham University and positive results about engagement, confidence and skills acquirement were reported. The children enjoyed the variety of activities and were made to feel successful and positive. This was an ideal app to use in partnership with parents and could be linked in with school activities very easily. Tangram is an app that was used as part of free play and a more structured game. The children were excited as when they combined shapes new shapes appeared and it worked well to give them free play before providing some more structured tasks. Sugar Smart is an app aiming at promoting healthy eating but can be used to develop numerical reasoning, number skills, measuring and data skills. The scanning of objects was fun with children trying to guess how many sugar cubes would appear. For the younger ones in the group this was guessing but this was an ideal working-in-partnership activity between teacher/parent and child and could be done in the home and also when out shopping. Some children in the group (not always the oldest) demonstrated strong data and sorting skills and translated the information well.

(Continued)

(Continued)

Table 7.2 Apps in action

App	Description	Activity
Maths 3–5 Maths 4–6	Takes children step by step through activities. It develops number recognition, sequencing skills, matching, mathematical vocabulary and shapes	There are 10 sections to each app which focus on different concepts. The app lends itself to individual working and working in pairs. This is an ideal application to recommend to parents Choose one of the sections for children to work through Allow children to work
Toca Store	Shopping game in which items must be matched and money counted	Toca games are play-focused and do not have scores. They allow children to create, work together and problem-solve This can be used without a formal plan and children were allowed to play and explore without instruction
Tayasui Tangram	Create animals out of differently shaped pieces	1. Challenge the children to build an animal with different rules • Free play • Provide a list of shapes that must be included • Provide a list of shapes and colours that must be used 2. Ask children to describe their animal to their partner and the shapes that are inside it
Sugar Smart	Scan barcodes on groceries to find out their sugar content. This can be done in the shop or at home	Items collected for scanning – tin of baked bean; carton of orange juice; packet of biscuits; yoghurt carton and pack of crisps Child scans each item and a visual of the amount of sugar in the item appears on the screen Older children can circle the number of sugar cubes opposite a picture of item on a worksheet Items can put in order of least to most sugar Tests mathematical reasoning and links to Health and Well-being

The apps can be used in both a structured and flexible manner against the skills and knowledge that are expected in both of the statutory frameworks. They can lead children into their Zone of Proximal Development (Vygotsky, 1978), i.e. the area between a child's level of independent performance (what he/she can do alone) and the child's level of assisted performance (what he/she can do with support). This case study used both structured and free play approaches to assess engagement, confidence and progress. They could also be easily extended to the home to enable parents to support their children's mathematical development. In terms of assessing engagement and understanding, each of the apps can be easily mapped onto the outcomes of the Foundation Stage and Foundation Phase (Table 7.3).

Table 7.3 Relating apps to the statutory frameworks in England and Wales

Foundation Phase (Wales)	Literacy and Numeracy Framework (Wales)	Foundation Stage (England)	Maths 3–5 Maths 4–6	Toca Store	Tayasui Tangram	Sugar Smart
Developing numerical reasoning	Developing numerical reasoning	Using mathematics in real-life situations	☆	☆		☆
Using number skills	Using number skills	Understanding number	☆	☆		☆
Using measuring skills	Using measuring skills	Measures	☆			☆
Using geometry skills		Shape and space	☆		☆	
Using data skills	Using data skills	Patterns and relationships	☆			☆

Theory into practice

The two case studies in this chapter are primarily based on the concept of how valuable social constructivism is to underpinning mathematical teaching in the Early Years curriculum. A key message in research into mathematical development is that attitude is everything in making children confident. Early encounters with mathematics develop confidence in their

Table 7.4 How the case studies link to the Foundation Phase and Foundation Stage

Foundation Phase	Foundation Stage	Case study 1	Case study 2
Personal and Social Development, Well-Being and Cultural Diversity	Personal, Social and Emotional Development	Foods sorted into healthy/unhealthy groups	Toca Shop – choosing items to buy, paying for items and role playing using mathematical vocabulary
Language, Literacy and Communication Skills	Communication and Language Literacy	Use of a book based on a counting game that goes from 10–1 and then 1–10	Tayasui Tangram Describing the shapes that were used to build the animal
Welsh Language Development		Using numbers in Welsh for activities	Opportunities for each of the apps to use Welsh vocabulary for numbers, shapes and role play
Mathematical Development	Mathematics	All areas in the frameworks covered	All areas in the frameworks covered
Knowledge and Understanding of the World	Understanding of the World	Measuring each other using the Lego bricks as a unit of measurement	Toca Shop – choosing items to buy, paying for items and role playing using mathematical vocabulary
Physical Development	Physical Development	Record the number of times you can clap when the ball is in the air Decorate polystyrene rings to look like a mouth and throw through coloured balls which are assigned different values	Maths 3–5 and Maths 4–6 – it is possible to link many of the challenges to physical activities
Creative Development	Expressive Arts and Design	Building a marble run with no instructions Using Lego bricks to build the tallest tower before falling down	Tayasui Tangram Creating animals out of different shapes, using camera function in app to capture

ability to understand and use mathematics. What these positive experiences do is help children to develop: curiosity, imagination, flexibility, inventiveness and persistence (Clements et al., 2004). In the case studies, practitioners and children were encouraged to be curious, creative and engage with a range of mathematical concepts. They were asked to talk about what they were doing when engaged with mathematical activities. This supported them to make sense of what they were doing.

Case studies 1 and 2 focus on three critical aspects of mathematical development in the early years: developing confident and creative practitioners in mathematics, encouraging digital literacy and involving parents in children's learning.

Both of the case studies are about providing tools to see the world through mathematical eyes and focus on important ideas. All of the activities were designed to enhance children's mathematical interest by connecting ideas to play and everyday life. There are excellent examples of ways in which we can build on children's mathematical thinking and how we can shift our focus onto the story and not just focus on the ending. A good example is the 'Let's Think!' approach used by one school, where children were encouraged to explain their thought processes, and to explore why they got things wrong – rather than being concerned that they had got these wrong (WAG, 2010).

Transitions and home–school links

In evaluations of the Foundation Phase (Wiserd, 2015) concerns have been expressed about the impact of a significant change in pedagogy, particularly in relation to numeracy and literacy where testing has been introduced. The Foundation Stage clearly explains what progression is expected from pupils as they moved from Early Years into Year 1 and 2 (DfE, 2014). An EYFS profile is completed on each child providing a holistic profile of knowledge, understanding and abilities, their progress against expected levels, and their readiness for Year 1. In England, there is a non-statutory guide for practitioners and inspectors to help inform understanding of children's mathematical development through the early years and expected outcomes (DfE, 2014). The expected outcomes before transition into Year 1 are as follows.

(Continued)

(Continued)

Numbers

Here children are required to count reliably from 1 to 20 and place numbers in order. They need to identify a number 1 below or 1 above a given number and solve problems such as halving and sharing. Children can use props such as objects to add and subtract two single-digit numbers and count on or back to find the answer to a given sum.

Shape, space and measures (SSM)

Within SSM children need to use everyday and mathematical language when they talk about size, weight, capacity, position, distance, time and money. Again they need to problem-solve and recognise and create patterns.

An evaluation of the pilot stage of the Foundation Phase in Wales was commissioned by the Welsh Government to explore the educational transitions for pupils aged 6–8, from the Foundation Phase to Key Stage 2. The research included a focused review of literature, in-depth case studies in 15 schools (involving pupil and teacher interviews and discussions) and a survey of all pilot and early start schools and a sample of non-pilot schools (WAG, 2010). Some concern was expressed about the different model of learning and interaction that children would meet in Year 2 but Estyn (2009) suggested that the practical skills developed in the Foundation Phase are particularly valuable in helping to raise boys' standards of achievements in mathematics. In relation to mathematics, the research found that children were positive and enthusiastic and that transition was being supported by ensuring that mathematics projects continued from the Foundation Phase to Year 2. On the negative side, there was concern about the introduction of Year 2 numeracy tests (Welsh Government, 2012).

For the Foundation Phase in Wales there is an overlap of two frameworks for practitioners to focus on – Early Years and the Literacy and Numeracy framework, which is ages 5–14 (Welsh Government, 2013). The mapping of the two frameworks had led to a clear transition to Year 1 and Year 2. Key features of the transition are:

- Progression can be demonstrated by more independence in problem-solving.
- Developing numerical reasoning, with the same elements running across Nursery to Year 2.

- Incremental increases in using number skills from Nursery to Year 2, with staged progression.
- Using measuring skills also follows an incremental development of concepts, moving from games to understanding measuring in meaningful contexts.
- Geometry skills focus on the same concepts from Nursery to Year 2 but increase in complexity.
- Data skills are taught through providing an underpinning of the two elements as complexity is increased but moving from collection in the Foundation Phase to analysis in Year 1/2.

The expected outcomes for mathematical development in the Foundation Phase were revised in 2015 and three overarching outcomes have been introduced and can be used for the end-of-phase assessment at the end of Year 2 (Welsh Government, 2015). The outcomes are measured as Bronze, Silver or Gold and move from simple counting and recognition to a more sophisticated application and understanding of concepts.

Jay, Rose and Simmons (2013; see also Rose et al., 2014) undertook a study of empowering parents to support their children's mathematics learning. The focus of the study was to look at mathematics as a part of everyday life. Although the main focus was Years 3 and 4, it has generated important findings for Early Years practitioners and generated practical resources. The key findings are:

- Using mathematics outside school can improve attitude and confidence in the concepts.
- Children need regular contact with mathematical concepts and this can be done in the home with guidance.
- Schools should explore ways in which they can work in partnership with parents. An important point made in the research is that this is not about parents having extensive mathematical knowledge. A key element is to talk with children and support the FS/FP aims of being able to talk about mathematical concepts.

Questions for your practice

[1] Which mathematical concepts do you find challenging to teach? Why is this so and how do you intend to overcome these challenges?

[2] How do you engage parents/carers when developing mathematical and numeracy skills in Early Years pupils?

(Continued)

(Continued)

[3] How do you ensure that you meet the goals outlined for the Foundation Phase/Early Years Foundation Stage?

[4] How do you incorporate technology into your teaching of mathematics?

Summary

The chapter has presented two case studies that focus on the very topical areas in Early Years education. They are:

- How do we develop practitioners' confidence in presenting mathematics in a positive, relevant, child-centred way that meets the outcomes of the two statutory frameworks?
- How do we involve parents in the Zone of Proximal Development?
- How do we use digital sources to encourage confidence, creativity and partnership learning?

Mathematics learning should be a positive environment for the teacher, parent and child. Our ability to engage with mathematical concepts can have a significant impact on our life chances. At the start of this chapter, the sobering figures about adult numeracy show that there are concerns about how we engage with mathematics and how the subject is perceived. However, the chapter also began with a positive statement about children's skills that can support mathematical learning development, such as curiosity, creativity and joy from such simple actions as stacking blocks. What is key is how we portray the subject and fundamentally how we establish a Zone of Proximal Development, which can guide and support the learner. Educators should be proactive and scaffold the learning in a way that is sympathetic to a learner's needs. We should aim to work in partnership and co-construct meaning with the child and often the parent too.

Recommendations for further reading

Boaler, J. (2010) *The Elephant in the Classroom: Helping Children Learn and Love Maths*. London: Souvenir Press. Maths can be fun if it is taught properly and this book explores positive ways to engage children with maths. It is full of positive and practical activities for the classroom and is underpinned by excellent research.

Dunphy, E., Dooley, T. and Shiel, G. (2014) *Mathematics in Early Childhood and Primary Education (3–8 years): Definitions, Theories, Development and Progression*. Available at: www.ncca.ie/en/Publications/Reports/NCCA_Research_Report_17.pdf (accessed 30 June 2016). An excellent review of research on mathematics learning of children aged 3–8 years presented in two reports. The first report (Research Report No. 17) focuses on theoretical aspects underpinning the development of mathematics education for young children. The second report (Research Report No. 18) is concerned with related pedagogical implications.

Dweck, Carol (2008) *Mindset and Math/Science Achievement. Teaching & Leadership: Managing for Effective Teachers and Leaders*. Available at: www.growthmindsetmaths.com/uploads/2/3/7/7/23776169/mindset_and_math_science_achievement_-_nov_2013.pdf (accessed 10 October 2016). Dweck is a leading psychologist in the field of personality and social psychology. The focus of the book is about developing confidence and positive mindsets in children, parents and teachers in relation to maths.

Hansen, A. (2011) *Games, Ideas and Activities for Early Years Mathematics (Classroom Gems)*. Harlow: Pearson Education. A great practical book providing easy-to-access and implement mathematical ideas for practitioners and teachers. The topics used are ideal for Early Years settings and classrooms, and fit well with the aims of the Foundation Phase and Foundation Stage.

References

Calder, N. (2011) *Processing Mathematics through Digital Technologies: The Primary Years*. Rotterdam: Sense Publishers.

Calder, N. (2015) 'Apps: Appropriate, applicable and appealing?', in T. Lowrie and R. Jorgensen (eds), *Digital Games and Mathematics Learning: Potential, Promises and Pitfalls*. Dordrecht: Springer. pp. 233–50.

Calder, N. and Campbell, A. (2016) 'Using mathematical apps with reluctant learners', *Digital Experiences in Mathematics Education*, 2 (1): 50–69.

Chinn, S. (2012) *More Trouble with Maths*. Wakefield: Egon Publishers.

Clements, D. H., Sarama, J. and DiBiase, A.-M. (eds) (2004) *Engaging Young Children in Mathematics: Standards for Early Childhood Mathematics*. Mahwah, NJ: Lawrence Erlbaum.

DCSF (2009) *Children Thinking Mathematically: PSRN Essential Knowledge for Early Years Practitioners*. Available at: www.childrens-mathematics.net/children thinkingmathematically_psrn.pdf (accessed 26 September 2016).

DfE (Department for Education) (2014) *Statutory Framework for the Early Years Foundation Stage: Setting the standards for learning, development and care for children from birth to five*. Available at: www.gov.uk/government/uploads/system/ uploads/attachment_data/file/335504/EYFS_framework_from_1_September_2014__ with_clarification_note.pdf (accessed 28 April 2017).

Estyn (2009) *Best Practice in Mathematics for Pupils Aged 3–7 Years*. Available at: www.estyn.gov.wales/sites/default/files/documents/Best%20practice%20in%20 mathematics%20for%20pupils%20aged%203%20to%207%20years%20-%20 June%202009.pdf (accessed 26 September 2016).

Ginsburg, H. (2009) 'Early mathematical education and how to do it', in O. Barbarin and B. Wasik (eds), *Handbook of Child Development and Early Education: Research to Practice*. New York: The Guilford Press. pp. 403–28.

Jay, T., Rose, J. and Simmons, B. (2013) 'Why parents can't get what they (think they) want'. Available at: www.bsrlm.org.uk/IPs/ip33-3/BSRLM-IP-33-3-06.pdf (accessed 26 September 2016).

Kuczera, M., Field, S. and Windisch, H. (2016) *Building Skills for All: A Review of England. Policy Insights from the Survey of Adult Skills*. Paris: OECD Publishing.

Nunes, T., Bryant, P., Sylva, K. and Barros, R. (2009) *Development of Maths Capabilities and Confidence in Primary School*. London: University of Oxford/DfE.

OECD (2013) *OECD Skills Outlook 2013: First Results from the Survey of Adult Skills*. Paris: OECD Publishing. Available at: http://dx.doi.org/10.1787/9789264204256-en.

Piaget, J. (1952) *The Origins of Intelligence in Children*. New York: International Universities Press.

Rose, J., Jay, T. and Simmons, B. (2014) 'It's helping your child experience the world: How parents can use everyday activities to engage their children in mathematical learning'. Presented at the European Conference of Educational Research, University of Porto, Portugal, 4 September.

Treffers, A. and Beishuizen, M. (1999) 'Realistic mathematics education in the Netherlands'. in I. Thompson (ed.), *Issues in Teaching Numeracy in Primary Schools*. Milton Keynes: Open University Press. pp. 27–38.

Vygotsky, L. (1978) *Mind in Society: The Development of Higher Psychological Processes*. Cambridge, MA: Harvard University Press.

WAG (Welsh Assembly Government) (2010) *Exploring Education Transitions for Pupils Aged 6–8 in Wales*. Cardiff: Welsh Assembly Government.

Welsh Government (2012) *National Numeracy Programme*. Cardiff: Welsh Government.

Welsh Government (2013) *National Literacy and Numeracy Framework*. Cardiff: Welsh Government.

Welsh Government (2015) *Curriculum for Wales: Foundation Phase Framework (revised 2015)*. Cardiff: Welsh Government. Available online at: http://gov.wales/ docs/dcells/publications/150803-fp-framework-en.pdf (accessed 28 April 2017).

Wiserd (2015) *Evaluating the Foundation Phase: Final Report*. Available at: http:// gov.wales/docs/caecd/research/2015/150514-foundation-phase-final-en.pdf (accessed 26 September 2017).

BECOMING A SCIENTIST THROUGH AN EXPERIENTIAL PEDAGOGY

Amanda Thomas, Karen Parker, Carole Carter and Clare Griffiths

Reading this chapter will help you to develop your knowledge and understanding of how practitioners teach young children science through an experiential pedagogy.

This chapter will:

- draw on two case studies, one in a Foundation Phase setting in a Welsh primary school with children aged 3–5 years and one in a day care setting with children aged 2–3 years
- focus on how an experiential pedagogy helps children develop their scientific knowledge and understanding and '*come to know*' the world through exploring different scientific concepts
- discuss how practitioners help children develop the skills of investigation and enquiry through a playful pedagogy

The Foundation Phase curriculum in Wales is for learners aged 3–7 years and has seven areas of learning, with science coming under Knowledge and Understanding of the World. The Foundation Phase documentation clearly advocates a cross-curricular approach to learning, with all seven areas of learning complementing each other and working together (WAG, 2008a).

The day care setting uses the 'Birth to Three Matters' framework for children aged 0 to 3 years. Again this is a holistic framework which has four aspects but it also recognises that learning and development needs to be all-inclusive (SureStart, 2002). As with the Foundation Phase, this framework is also cross-curricular.

The adults in both settings support the children through communication, co-construction of knowledge, listening and asking open-ended questions. In both settings the children are assessed through observation whilst investigating the properties of different materials and taking ownership of their scientific explorations.

Key words

experiential, coconstructing, exploration, enquiry, investigating, communicating, sorting, predicting, experimenting, reflecting

Theoretical perspectives

Science is a subject that lends itself very well to a skills-based approach to learning. It is a subject that children naturally 'learn by doing', especially in the investigation part of the science curriculum. Children are naturally curious and are active explorers; by enabling and supporting this curiosity we help children to develop deeper thinking skills. Through experiential activities children are able to enhance their cognitive development, communication skills and scientific understanding through the development of thinking skills. As Johnston (2014) argues, children need to take ownership and be active in gathering understanding of the world we live in. They need to do this by building upon previous experience and knowledge (Piaget, 1929). Science is all about testing out ideas and theories and communicating with each other, whilst becoming scientific thinkers and pioneers.

Science begins with children exploring the world around them and scientific knowledge involves the construction of meaning (Clarke and Phethean, 2011). If children are given appropriate investigative activities and work with supportive adults then children will communicate their ideas in a scientific way (Pulham, 1998; also Clarke, 2003). Children need space and time to think and interact with their environment and adults.

Harlen and Qualter (2014: 98) argue that in science there are 'four main groups of skills that can be described as "science enquiry"'. These can be summarised as:

- asking questions, predicting and planning investigations
- gathering evidence by observing and using information sources
- analysing, interpreting and explaining
- communicating, arguing, reflecting and evaluating

In the Foundation Phase guidance for the Knowledge and Understanding of the World area of learning it states that, 'Children will be provided with meaningful experiences … they will undertake investigations that engage their interests' (WAG, 2008a: 4). The 'Birth to Three Matters' framework for children advocates teaching skills and competences through an approach of investigation and exploration of the world, and through collaboration with others (SureStart, 2002). Both these documents advocate a hands-on, active approach to scientific enquiry and exploration.

In both settings used for this chapter, children are assessed through observation. This is because, as the Welsh Assembly Government state, 'By observing children while they are involved in activities, practitioners will find out how the children's skills are developing and what they are able to do' (WAG, 2008b: 4). This is evident in both case studies detailed in this chapter, where the practitioners observe the children and allow time for them to investigate the materials on offer.

Science can be considered to require the development of the following skills:

- Exploration
- Investigation
- Enquiry

In order to understand how these skills relate to science it is necessary to clarify what each skill actually means. One definition of *exploration*, as offered by Howe et al. (2005), is that of investigating and exploring different objects, whereas Johnston (2014) argues that exploring skills are made up of observation, raising questions and classifying. *Investigation* is more goals-orientated than exploration and encourages questions and allows children to work in groups or independently. It allows children to plan and obtain evidence to test out ideas (Davies and Howe, 2007). *Enquiry* encompasses both exploration and investigation – it is what scientists do, investigating and exploring using scientific methods (Johnston, 2014). The three skills are described in more detail in what follows.

For our youngest learners exploratory play is most often associated with scientific development (Johnston, 2005). Exploration motivates children as it encourages engagement in scientific processes such as observations and investigations (Johnston, 2014). The Foundation Phase curriculum for 3-to-7-year-olds is defined as being holistic, with learning through play provided by first-hand experiential activities (WAG, 2008a). This supports the exploratory nature of science activities. The 'Birth to Three Matters' framework for 0 to 3-year-olds is a *'hands on'* learning curriculum that supports active learning through play, again supporting the exploratory nature of scientific investigations.

As stated previously, investigating is what scientists do. In both case studies the children are investigating different scientific phenomena. The children work in small groups but also have time to investigate the materials independently. They use observation, communication and reflection to carry out their investigations successfully. The adults are on hand to support and guide the children in their construction and development of knowledge and understanding.

With scientific enquiry, Harlen (2006) argues that children need to develop scientific literacy and that scientific enquiry is central to this. When engaged in the process of scientific enquiry children are using their skills of observation, predicting and interpreting (Clarke and Phethean, 2011). Practitioners have a responsibility to become scientific facilitators, allowing children to work with their peers, to explore and discover new ways of thinking and learning whilst offering support and guidance if needed. They need to be confident in their own scientific knowledge and be prepared to carry on developing their knowledge as needed. Practitioners can be supported in this through INSET days within their own schools where they disseminate good practice in science. Practitioners can also attend training courses and workshops on delivering science provided by external providers. Finally, schools can also be part of professional learning communities (PLCs) where they join with other schools to share good practice and ideas on specific subject areas such as science.

The role of the adult

Practitioners need to be good role models during scientific explorations and encourage and support the children. This can be through 'playing' alongside the children or asking appropriate open ended questions and giving children the time and space to think. Again this can be seen in the case studies for this chapter where the adults are co-constructing knowledge alongside the children by asking questions and listening to the children's responses.

This process of asking questions, observing and listening to children's responses links into the theories of Vygotsky (1896–1934). Vygotsky believed that children needed to talk about their thoughts and ideas with interested adults. He stated that children are active in their learning and practitioners need to observe children carefully to see what they can or cannot do and plan a curriculum accordingly (Pound, 2006). Vygotsky also believed children could learn from each other with more able children or adults scaffolding the learning of less able children. This is supported by Bruner (1991), who stated that active social interaction with children learning alongside their peers appears to be the most effective means of early scientific learning. Bruner (1986, as cited in Gray and MacBlain, 2015) and Vygotsky (1978) both believed that teachers play an essential role in developing children's thinking and learning (Gray and MacBlain, 2015). In dialogic teaching the teachers and children share ideas equally and communication can support cognitive development (Mercer, 2000). In both settings used in this chapter the practitioners were very much part of the children's learning journeys. They encouraged group interaction and ensured every child had the opportunity to take an equal part in the activities.

This appears in contrast to the theories of Piaget (1929), who placed little emphasis on the role of the teacher. He coined the term 'lone scientist' when describing a child who learns through practical experience and argued that children learn through self-discovery (Gray and MacBlain, 2015). For Piaget, the teacher's role was to solely provide and manage a suitable learning environment. However, for Vygotsky, the teacher had a central role, leading children to new levels of understanding through social interactions (Hodson, 1999).

The following case studies are examples of the exploratory, experiential pedagogical approach to science as advocated by both the FP and the 'Birth to Three Matters' curriculum framework. Both investigations stimulate children's curiosity and motivate their interests, and knowledge is co-constructed by supportive adults.

Case studies

Case study 1: Melting ice

In the day care setting children aged 2–3 years are investigating the properties of ice for their topic 'At the seaside'. The practitioner has frozen water and rice, dyed blue with food colouring, into rectangular blocks of ice which she adds to the water tray. The children are asked to explore the ice through touch, talk and questioning. They spend some time feeling the ice and they tell each other it feels cold. Next the children are asked to poke, prod and listen to the ice as the practitioner adds warm blue water to the water tray. Throughout, the practitioner asks the children questions about what is happening and listens to their responses. The children squeal with delight as the ice cracks and keep asking for more blue water to be added. Throughout the children share their understanding by using vocabulary such as 'cold', 'blue' and 'wet' and 'hard'. The children feel the rice as the ice melts and say it is 'bumpy'; the practitioner tells them it feels like sand at the seaside. They spend some time simply watching and feeling the ice melt away to reveal the 'blue' rice inside.

Case study 2: Floating and sinking

In a Foundation Phase setting, 3- and 4-year-olds are investigating floating and sinking as part of their topic 'Land Ahoy'. Children are working with the practitioner to predict and investigate which objects will float and sink in a bowl of water placed on the table. Before they start the practitioner reminds the children the learning outcome of the activity: To find out which objects float or sink. She recaps words linked to floating and sinking, building upon the children's prior knowledge. She reminds them of a short video clip they watched earlier that explored things that float and things that sink. She asks the children to remind her of some of the objects seen in the video and whether or not they floated or sank.

Next the practitioner explains the practical activity. She allows the children time to feel each of the objects and to discuss with her and each other whether they think they will float or sink once added to the water. The children initially sort the objects into two hoops labelled

'Float' and 'Sink' and the practitioner takes a photo of their predictions. This is then printed off for comparison with the actual test results.

The children take it in turns to add an object to the bowl of water to test if their predictions were correct. They then sort the objects once more into the two hoops, discussing their findings. They reflect on whether or not their initial predictions were correct, using the original photograph to help them. Throughout the activity the teacher asks the children questions about their findings and asks them to explain the results in their own words.

To finish, the children complete a worksheet of the activity where they tick if an object floats or sinks based on their findings. The teacher takes a photograph as evidence of their final results.

Theory into practice

In both the case studies in this chapter the children are learning through experiential, real-life activities. In the case of the ice and water, the practitioners ensure the children are engaged by keeping their interest throughout by asking questions. The children are not rushed through the activity but are given time to feel the ice and the rice and to respond to the questions. They are learning about the properties of ice and water and the whole activity is linked to a real-life scenario of being at the seaside.

In the second case study the children have already been given some prior knowledge of floating and sinking and the practical activity is used to consolidate and expand on their knowledge and understanding. Again the practitioner facilitates understanding through questioning the children, making those vital links between theory and practice. The children are able to use the skills of predicting and then testing their hypotheses to see if their predictions were correct.

Since 2008 the Welsh Government has broken away from the rest of the UK in its education delivery. The Foundation Phase (FP) for 3-to-7-year-olds has been introduced as a child-centred and experiential pedagogy where children learn through play. The implementation of this play-based curriculum required a shift in focus from an adult-led, didactic approach to a much more shared ethos, where the practitioner and child work together using an experiential pedagogy.

Children learn best through an experiential approach where they are given opportunities to construct their knowledge and ideas in a supportive framework. They learn through interaction with their peers, exploring their natural curiosity and voicing their thoughts and ideas. By practitioners providing children with activities that foster this sense of discovery, engage their curiosity and provide stimulation and excitement, children develop their reasoning skills and build up their knowledge and understanding of the world. This is congruent with Russell and McGuigan (2016), who write that children are active learners who learn about the world, people and the environment from actively engaging with it.

Practitioners support young children in coming to know through experiential activities that link into the skills and range for science within the curriculum being studied (Birth to Three Matters in Case study 1 and Foundation Phase (FP) in Case study 2). Examples of science activities include investigating how materials change through heating and cooling; teaching children to explore simple life cycles of plants and animals, whilst noting differences between themselves and other organisms and sorting objects according to similarities and differences; and exploring different sources of light and sound (Welsh Government, 2015). From these activities children are gaining skills of exploring and experimenting, questioning and listening. They are encouraged to ask 'what if?' and to predict and to communicate their observations and findings.

The case studies discussed in this chapter develop these skills, with children and practitioners in both the day care setting and the FP setting working in partnership to explore and investigate scientific principles and concepts. Here children in Case study 2 are meeting the requirements of the 'Knowledge and Understanding of the World' area of learning within the FP by 'Experiment[ing] with different everyday materials and us[ing] their senses to sort them into groups according to simple properties' (Welsh Government, 2015: 42).

In the day care setting the investigation of melting ice (Case study 1) fits under all four aspects of the 'Birth to Three Matters', where the children were 'Finding out what s/he can do'; 'Exploring, experimenting, labelling and expressing'; 'Exploring and discovering'; and 'Acquiring physical skills' (SureStart, 2002: 7).

Science as part of the curriculum has always lent itself to '*learning by doing*' and children are actively encouraged to take ownership of their own learning and to engage in dialogue with their peers, whilst testing out new ideas and concepts. As Loxley et al. (2014) state, all scientific activities require enquiry and discovery.

By giving children experiential activities we enable them to enhance and develop their cognitive and scientific understanding. Pulham (1998) and

Clarke (2003) researched children's understandings of materials and found that, if given an appropriate context and opportunities, even the youngest children are willing to communicate their scientific ideas. This can be seen in the case studies where young children are able to use key scientific vocabulary and concepts through communicating that the ice has melted to being able to discuss which objects float and sink.

When investigating the properties of ice and water in Case study 1 the children are communicating their thoughts and ideas to each other and each contribution is valued. Here the children are encouraged to use their senses to investigate what the water and ice feel like and how the rice feels once the ice has melted. They use their senses to explore and investigate at first hand how the materials feel and how they change when warm water is added to the ice (as shown in Figure 8.1a).

The practitioners are keen to encourage all the children to take part and continually ask the children open questions such as: 'How does the ice feel?' 'Is it cold?' 'What is happening when we add the warm water?' 'How can we get the rice out?' The children respond with, 'It is cold.' 'It feels squashy.' 'The rice is bumpy like the sand.' 'More blue water?' 'It is the sea, I like the sea.' The practitioners reinforce the scientific concepts throughout by stating that the 'Ice has melted' and that the warm water has caused the ice to 'melt.' Children are drawing on prior experiences by remembering their own visits to the seaside, activities already under-taken in the home and in the setting, and are able to describe how the rice feels by comparing it to sand.

In Case study 2 the children are encouraged to predict which of the objects will float or sink prior to starting the investigation (as shown in Figure 8.1b). Before starting the investigation the practitioner reinforces the learning outcome for the activity. In the Foundation Phase setting this is done when the children are told what they are going to learn (learning objective). The practitioner also tells the children about the success criteria for the activity. This method of introducing the learning objective and suc-cess criteria at the start of activities is used throughout the Foundation Phase, providing consistency for the children. The learning objective for this activity is to investigate and explore which objects float or sink, and the success criteria for the children are being able to identify and sort out which objects float and sink.

In advance of the practical part of the investigation, the practitioner asks the children to explain to her what the terms floating and sinking mean based on prior teaching. The children give a range of responses including, *'When you stay on top of the sea,'* and *'When you are above the water.'*

The children have previously read books on floating and sinking and have watched a video clip reinforcing the concept. The practitioner asks each child in turn to sort out the objects into sets of objects that either float or sink. Each child is encouraged to voice their predictions and to take a turn in sorting the objects. The teacher takes a picture of the children's predictions as in the FP children's work needs to be evidenced using a range of methods. Then she asks them to test if their predictions were correct by adding the objects to the water to see if they float or sink. The practitioner reinforces the scientific vocabulary of floating and sinking and discusses with the children why certain materials float and why some do not in terms that are understandable to the children.

The children are then asked to once more sort the objects into those that float and those that sink, reflecting upon their experiment. The results are compared with the original picture, allowing the children to reflect upon their findings. The children record their findings onto a worksheet by ticking float or sink for each object (as shown in Figure 8.1c).

For the rest of the week the children were given access to the water tray during free choice activities and provided with a range of resources to add to the water to continue exploring floating and sinking. In this way they were able to consolidate their learning in their free play. Adults were on hand to reinforce the vocabulary of floating and sinking with the children and they spent time observing the children as they worked independently and together.

In the Foundation Phase and the day care setting children will revisit topics building upon prior knowledge. This is what Janet Moyles terms the 'play spiral'. In her seminal book *Just Playing?* (1989) she advocates that

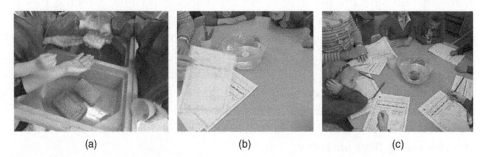

(a)   (b)   (c)

Figure 8.1a   Multi-sensory exploration of ice, rice and warm water

Figure 8.1b   Predicting which objects will float or sink

Figure 8.1c   Children recording their findings

children need free play sessions to explore objects and then they can work with a practitioner in a directed play task, developing new knowledge and understanding. Now when the children revisit the same task or activity during free play they will apply that new knowledge and understanding. Bruner (1960) talked of the concept of the spiral curriculum. Here, information is structured so that more complex ideas can be taught at an easier level first, and then revisited at more complex levels later on. Teaching in this way should allow children to develop the skills of being able to solve problems by themselves (Mcleod, 2012).

Both case studies outlined in this chapter support Moyles' play spiral and Bruner's spiral curriculum. Here the children were given time to play with the resources on offer before, during and after the activities. There were opportunities in both the FP setting and the day care setting for the children to revisit the activities offered throughout the week and again during the year. In addition, as the children move up classes in the FP or into different rooms in the day care setting the concept of materials and their properties would be revisited at a more complex level. Here the children would be able to apply their prior understanding, allowing them to develop more complex knowledge and skills.

Scientific enquiry was evident in both case studies, allowing learning to take place by giving the children first-hand experiences. In each example from the FP and the day care setting practitioners were careful to engage the children in open dialogue before, during and after the experiments. The practitioners encouraged the children to think of themselves as independent learners and thinkers, as well as collaborative partners throughout the science lessons. They fostered a dialogic teaching approach where the children shared thoughts and ideas on an equal footing throughout the activities (Mercer, 2000). Communication became a two-way process with the practitioners discussing scientific concepts and hypotheses with the children, which as Cazden (2001) points out, can aid cognitive development and develop thinking skills. Bruner (1991) also supports this pedagogical approach by arguing that children should learn alongside peers as an effective means of scientific learning. The children were encouraged to communicate verbally, through their written work and their drawings. In studying science children, even in their early years, employ a range of skills to take ownership of their understanding or 'coming to know'. Children employ lines of enquiry that lead to a knowledge and understanding of the world.

In the case studies described the children have been asked questions or are asking questions of the teacher and each other. They are observing and using information and they are explaining in their own words what they think is happening. Communication and scientific enquiry are evident in both case studies and the children are given the time to reflect upon their findings. Loxley et al. (2014) attest that children need to talk about a concept to understand it. By linking theory to practice in this way, children are '*coming to know*' their world and to develop their understanding of scientific concepts.

Transition and home–school links

Children are naturally curious and this curiosity needs to be harnessed in the early years and onwards. Oliver (2006) attests that children have a need and want to understand the world. Practitioners need to be aware that children will already have ideas about the world around them and how things work. By working closely with the children and their parents, practitioners can meet and match children's learning needs, building on what they already know.

In the day care setting children's developments are evidenced in each child's development book and when a child has securely achieved a skill it is crossed off and dated and the next steps identified. These books are passed on to the next practitioner and a copy given to parents so they are able to see what they child has achieved and what they will be concentrating on next. The day care setting holds regular open days where the parents can come in and talk to the staff about their child's progress and each day a communication diary is sent home where staff note what the children have done that day. This encourages the parents to develop children's knowledge and understanding at home, building upon the activities the children have undertaken in the day care setting. In addition, by having an open door policy the setting is able to communicate in an open and friendly manner with parents to build upon the activities the children have undertaken at home. This allows children to settle in more quickly and ease transitions from home to the setting.

Science lends itself well to translating activities undertaken at home into the setting; examples can include:

- bath time – opportunities for floating and sinking
- baking – how materials change properties when heated
- gardening – life cycles of plants

In the day care setting staff hold regular meetings with each other and discuss their observations of the children. Children are allocated key workers who liaise with the parents and will discuss the children in their care with the next key worker when the children are ready to move on. There is continual open communication and continuity of care, with regular visits from a Foundation Phase (FP) teacher to prepare any children who will be moving next into a school setting. The day care setting ensures that the children's individual development books are sent on to any new settings as well as any other relevant information as required. Within the individual development books there is evidence of children's achievements in all four aspects of the 'Birth to Three Matters' framework, which are dated and signed. There are also details of observations carried out including those linked to science and details of the next steps required.

In the FP setting there is a transition day where all staff meet to discuss the new children moving into their class. Here, children's achievements are evidenced in individual portfolios and, for 'Knowledge and Understanding of the World', they will have been awarded a Foundation Phase outcome by the previous teacher, using a 'best fit' criterion based on observations throughout the year. Obstacles to transition such as different pedagogical approaches should not be an issue for children moving classes in the FP as it is a learning continuum for ages 3 to 7 years. Here practitioners are using the same framework for learning and are building upon the same seven areas of learning and FP outcomes from previous years. This means in practice that children will revisit topics in subsequent years building upon the knowledge and understanding already gained. Transition should be seen as a process and not an event, with a good partnership between professionals and parents (Johnston, 2014). Children also spend a day in their new class before the end of the summer term so in the September of the next academic year it will not seem so daunting.

Transition needs to be handled carefully to ensure that any new learning takes into account prior knowledge and builds upon that (Trodd, 2013). According to Dowling (1995), we need to get it right at an early age otherwise transitions can have an effect on learning

(Continued)

(Continued)

for life. Both the settings discussed in this chapter have transition procedures in place and encourage collaboration between staff and parents and carers.

In the FP setting the children regularly take home their 'Learning Logs'. In these there are activities for the children to complete at home with the parents. These are returned to the setting to be marked by the practitioners the following week. In this way the parents can see what topics the children have been studying and can support these at home. In both settings parents are welcome to come in and talk to the practitioners about their children and to look at any work they have completed.

Questions for your practice

[1] How do you plan for scientific enquiry in your setting – are the children given lots of hands-on opportunities?
[2] Are the children given opportunities and time to simply explore materials and resources with or without an adult being present?
[3] Do you actively encourage independence and group work during science investigations?
[4] How do you assess if the children are developing scientific literacy and are 'coming to know' the world around them?

Summary

Today, the debate still rages over how best to teach science but certainly in Wales the emphasis is on incorporating an experiential, enquiry-based approach from the earliest stages. The play-based approach of the Foundation Phase for learners aged 3 to 7 years and the 'birth to three' framework used in the day care setting allow our youngest learners to explore and investigate scientific principles co-constructively with their peers. This fits in with the ethos of both frameworks as being holistic and child-centred.

Science is all about testing out ideas and theories and communicating with each other, whilst encouraging children to become scientific thinkers and pioneers. Practitioners have a responsibility to become scientific facilitators, allowing children to work with their peers, to explore and discover new ways of thinking and learning whilst offering support and guidance if needed. This links into the theories of Vygotsky (1896–1934), who believed that children needed to talk about their thoughts and ideas with interested adults. He stated that children are active in their learning and practitioners need to observe children carefully to see what they can or cannot do and plan a curriculum accordingly (Pound, 2006). Vygotsky also believed children could learn from each other, with more able children or adults scaffolding the learning of less able children. Children need time to play with and investigate resources and to come up with their own hypotheses to test. By allowing children the freedom to play with resources and come up with their own ways of 'coming to know', a positive learning environment is created.

In all the case studies discussed there is active dialogue between the children and the practitioner. Each practitioner has been careful to ensure that the science investigations on offer stimulate the children's natural curiosity and that the children are given time to explore the available resources. Through the shared discussions and negotiations that follow children are developing their scientific knowledge and skills. Practitioners are eager and enthusiastic to share this learning journey with the children in their care and to provide them with the experiential opportunities that allow them to 'come to know' the world around them.

Recommendations for further reading

Dunne, M. and Peacock, A. (eds) (2012) *Primary Science*. London: Sage. This book gives ideas and ways to implement science teaching in the primary classroom.

Johnston, J. (2014) *Emergent Science*. Abingdon: Routledge. This text supports the teaching of science from birth to 8 years old and draws on the theory and skills required to develop a knowledge and understanding of science for our youngest learners.

Peacock, G., Sharp, J., Johnsey, R. and Wright, D. (2012) *Primary Science: Knowledge and Understanding*, 6th edn. London: Learning Matters.

Consolidates a knowledge and understanding of primary science across a range of key topics.

Russell, T. and McGuigan, L. (2016) *Exploring Science with Young children.* London: Sage. A really useful text for practitioners working with children in the Early Years as it explores scientific concepts and activities by linking theory to practice.

References

Bruner, J. (1960) *The Process of Education.* Cambridge, MA: Harvard University Press.

Bruner, J. (1991) 'The narrative construction of reality', *Critical Inquiry*, 18 (1): 1–21.

Cazden, C. (2001) *Classroom Discourse: The Language of Learning and Teaching.* Portsmouth: Heinemann.

Clarke, H. (2003) 'Encouraging young children to talk about materials: reflections on the influence of context on young children's expression and development of scientific ideas', PhD thesis, University of Southampton.

Clarke, H. and Phethean, K. (2011) 'Encouraging enquiry: Exploring the world around us', in J. Georgeson, J. Moyles and J. Payler (eds), *Beginning Teaching, Beginning Learning in Early Years and Primary Education.* Maidenhead: Open University Press.

Davies, D. and Howe, A. (2007) 'Exploration, investigation and enquiry', in J. Moyles (ed.), *Beginning Teaching, Beginning Learning*, 3rd edn. Maidenhead: McGraw–Hill. pp. 74–85.

Dowling, M. (1995) *Starting School at Four: A Joint Endeavour.* London: Paul Chapman Publishing.

Gray, C. and MacBlain, S. (2015) *Learning Theories in Childhood.* London: Sage.

Harlen, W. (2006) *Teaching, Learning and Assessing Science 5–12*, 4th edn. London: Sage.

Harlen, W. and Qualter, A. (2014) *The Teaching of Science in Primary Schools*, 6th edn. London: Routledge.

Hodson, D. (1999) 'Building a case for a sociocultural and inquiry orientated view of science education', *Journal of Science Education and Technology*, 8 (3): 241–9.

Howe, A., Davies, D., McMahon, K., Towler, L. and Scott, T. (2005) *Science 5–11: A Guide for Teachers.* London: David Fulton.

Johnston, J. (2005) *Early Explorations in Science*, 2nd edn. Milton Keynes: Open University Press.

Johnston, J. (2014) *Emergent Science.* London: Routledge.

Loxley, P., Dawes, L., Nicholls, L. and Dores, B. (2014) *Teaching Primary Science*, 2nd edn. London: Routledge.

Mcleod, S. (2012) *Bruner.* Available at: www.simplypsychology.org/bruner.html (accessed 20 August 2015).

Mercer, N. (2000) *Words and Minds.* London: Routledge.

Moyles, J. (1989) *Just Playing? Role and Status of Play in Early Childhood Education.* Milton Keynes: Open University Press.

Oliver, A. (2006) *Creative Teaching Science.* London: Fulton.

Piaget, J. (1929) *The Child's Conception of the World.* New York: Harcourt.

Pound, L. (2006) *How Children Think and Learn.* London: Step Forward Publishing.

Pulham, S. M. (1998) 'Developing and using a range of contexts to explore young children's ideas about materials'. MPhil thesis, King Alfred's College, Winchester.

Russell, T. and McGuigan, L. (2016) *Exploring Science with Young Children.* London: Sage.

SureStart (2002) *Birth to Three Matters: An Introduction to the Framework.* London: SureStart.

Trodd, L. (2013) *Transitions in the Early Years.* London: Sage.

Vygotsky, L. (1978) *Mind in Society: The Development of Higher Psychological Processes.* Cambridge, MA: Harvard University Press.

WAG (Welsh Assembly Government) (2008a) *Knowledge and Understanding of the World.* Cardiff: Welsh Assembly Government.

WAG (Welsh Assembly Government) (2008b) *Observing Children.* Cardiff: Welsh Assembly Government.

Welsh Government (2015) *Framework for Children's Learning for 3–7-year-olds in Wales (revised 2015).* Cardiff: Welsh Assembly Government.

INSPIRING CREATIVITY IN THE EARLY YEARS

Catherine Jones and Francine Davies

Reading this chapter will help you to understand:

- how to capture individual creativity in an Early Years environment
- how to use a creative concept to develop motor skills, literacy, turn ideas into objects and work together on a shared experience
- how creativity can foster confidence in children and parents
- how Early Years practitioners, service providers, children and parents can work creatively together

Creativity is a very natural thing, enabling exploration, experimentation, problem-solving and enjoyment. The aim of this chapter is to look at creativity through knowledge and self-expression and how we can generate environments for creativity to flourish both in school and in the home. Creativity is a key theme in both the Foundation Phase (Wales) and the Early Years Foundation Stage (England); in Wales it is Creative Development and in England it is Expressive Arts and Design. Creativity is really a process and sometimes there is no clear output or product. What both the Foundation Phase (FP) and Early Years Foundation Stage (EYFS) emphasise is its role in terms of building children's confidence and skills in learning.

Key words

self-expression, confidence, experimentation, curiosity, creativity across the curriculum, inclusivity

Theoretical perspectives

Mellou (1996) suggests that young children's creativity can be nurtured through educational settings in three respects: the creative environment, creative programmes and creative teachers in their ways of teaching. The Foundation Phase curriculum (Welsh Government, 2015) has knowledge and self-expression at its heart whilst the Foundation Stage (DfE, 2014) focuses on expressive arts and design with its two key concepts being Exploring Using Media and Materials and Being Imaginative. Thus, storytelling and creative crafts are a useful infrastructure to build upon. The connection between the art of storytelling and the art of creative craft has the potential to encourage creative thought. This combination, if delivered sensitively, can facilitate a respect for listening and encourage the exploration of thought processes through discussion and experimentation with language. Therefore, the introduction of creative crafts to support a story has the potential to reinforce these intentions and allow motor-skills to be exercised.

What do we mean by creativity? A number of words readily come to mind: imagination; originality; problem-solving and production. Everyone has the potential to express themselves creatively if given an opportunity. However, what holds individuals back is an assumption that there is a correct creative, visual outcome to be achieved. As practitioners we have the opportunity to provide learners with the skills and a framework of reference that can inspire creative development. We can do this in many ways, e.g. showing learners that we value difference and the different perspectives that each of us project in our lives, offering a unique point of view. From birth, a child begins to develop a mental map with reference points mainly comprised of the influential group of people that form their world. That is not to say that even from birth the child does not have a key involvement in the development of their world but more often decisions are made for them rather than by them, but children will be actively reacting not purely passively receiving. The children that we work with as Early Years practitioners will arrive with a diverse map of their own and a wide spectrum of ability and desire to express their experiences, whether intentionally or unintentionally. For these reasons it becomes paramount that we acknowledge the value of each individual perspective and mental map. An understanding of the individual's map will provide the landmark from which to begin our relationship and journey as a learner and class member. As educational practitioners we are striving not only to listen to the voices of our recipients but also to impart knowledge and learning in the process.

Prentice (2000) suggests that active involvement from children, teacher and parents is vital for creativity to flourish in an educational setting. All participants in this relationship need to be actively involved in the process of shared learning. Research has also shown that it is possible for adults to help children improve their imaginative play skills, with apparent positive consequences for their creative abilities (Russ, 2003). As practitioners we argue that by appreciating and celebrating difference and not focusing on perfection we are providing a stimulating, safe framework within which learners can interpret and express ideas. Such an opportunity allows children to explore rather than strive to measure their ideas against a predetermined end result or product. Working creatively in this manner can be liberating and enables us to take risks rather than holding back just in case it does not turn out right. As an artist exploring the fundamentals of art practice, I am reminded of the potential freedoms and uninhibited, boundless mind of a child when drawing and painting. When an adult is required to consider composition in a picture often a complex set of parameters will intrude and guide the outcome. However, children can be acknowledged for their skill at achieving exemplary composition as a result of the freedom and instinctive mark-making they practise. There is considerable research that seeks to explain how and why this perception can be lost as a child develops into adulthood, but in this instance I would simply like to acknowledge its existence and value as a means of highlighting how an awareness of it has huge potential for creative practice.

Therefore, taking these two inspirations on board brings with it a freedom to experiment and become excited by the possibility of what may occur given an opportunity to have a go. However, for practitioners, such

Table 9.1 Aims of the workshops by stakeholders

Service providers	Children	Parents/guardians/practitioners
To increase awareness among users of the integrated Children's Centre of accessible, creative tools that can facilitate a lifelong approach to learning and creative thought	To give the children the opportunity to be actively creative irrespective of their age or ability	To enable and create confidence among Early Years practitioners and adults engaging with Early Years to integrate creative and experiential tools and techniques into their work with children
To use a creative toolkit to facilitate an effective working relationship between service users	To develop awareness of the creative opportunities in everyday life by introducing no cost, easily accessible materials thus encouraging the longevity of impact of the creative experience	
	To engage children in the act of listening through use of interactive storytelling	
	The use of stimulating props and well-planned activities to engage children's curiosity and make them feel confident to explore and process their own creative thoughts and actions	

an awareness of the resulting philosophy in practice, whilst liberating, is not without its conundrums. The idea of experimenting and taking risks and chances when working with children and others carries with it a number of extra considerations, the most obvious being the need to act safely and responsibly. However, that should become a predetermined stage in the process rather than a factor that inhibits the creativity. Being in charge of what you are seeking to achieve in a creative project ensures a degree of certainty in the outcome but by the nature of working with others through the reliance on their behaviour, will inevitably leave a small amount to chance. This element of organised chaos that as practitioners we have to master can be daunting. Yet, a series of questions can be explored thoroughly during preparatory stages to manage the outcomes of chance. Whilst the following questions are not finite they can stimulate further thought and actions. The next part of this chapter focuses on two case studies of creativity in practice in an Early Years setting. To help your understanding of the case studies, the overarching aims of the works are explained.

Case studies

Case study 1: Engaging children in the creative world

Integrated Children's Centres (ICC) provide an integrated service to secure good outcomes for children and their parents, focusing on providing the best start in life,

The Integrated Children's Centre in the case studies consisted of a bilingual nursery, a pre-school nursery and a Flying Start nursery offering free childcare for two and a half hours a day (Flying Start is part of the Welsh Government Early Years programme for families with children under 4 years of age living in disadvantaged areas of Wales). All three nurseries were working towards a Foundation Phase curriculum and in addition to childcare provision the centre provided additional services for parents, guardians and carers. Whilst the case studies focus on children aged 2 and above, within this setting younger siblings were involved during work with parents/guardians. A holistic approach was decided on to ensure the most effective use of time, resources and the inclusivity of all centre users. The workshops would introduce the creative model in the first instance and then be tailored to fit the Learning Objectives being addressed in each setting.

It was agreed that each service provider would be allocated a day for a creative, storytelling workshop. This would enable all children and staff to fully participate in the creative workshops and for each setting to be able to continue with day-to-day functions relatively easily. The workshop would consist of a group of between four and eight children at a time and two members of staff. Sixty minutes were allocated per workshop and approximately four were undertaken throughout the day.

The World of Ogs is a creative concept developed to help practitioners working with children to express themselves creatively through play and creative activity. The concept consists of props and original stories motivated by a common theme, namely, helping children to celebrate difference and aiming to encourage active engagement with the world around them.

The props include a set of characters made out of old clothes, an old, vintage suitcase in which they travel, a willow tipi which represents their home, a series of furniture and utensils made out of old bits of wood, jam jar lids, shells and so forth, all of which help express the environmentally friendly ethos behind the concept.

The following short rhyme is read at the start with the sole aim of opening up a world of unimaginable possibilities to the children. Fundamental to this stage is creating a sense of drama for the audience. Imagine the children are about to see a performance and you the practitioner are the performer!

'Ever wondered why moths find your woolly jumpers delicious?
Or why blankets that look soft are so itchy it's hideous!
Or if one sock goes missing it returns covered in fluff!
Then meet The Ogs who know about this stuff!'

Engaging the children as soon as they enter the workshop was important and was achieved using high-visibility props. A large shape covered by a considerable, colourful, crocheted blanket and a pile of old clothes on the floor are easily noticed. The children are both curious and excited. The story being read to the children immediately introduces further props and questions to keep their attention. The children have the opportunity to touch things, hear things and wonder about things. They notice new things and begin to explore and question what is in front of them.

It is children's willingness to pretend in their play that allows the arms of jumpers to be readily accepted as a trunk of an elephant and the teeth on a zip to be considered as the teeth of a crocodile and so on. The story unfolds introducing the characters and encourages the children to engage with the funny names, the likes and dislikes all of which give them personality. When the characters are found in the piles of clothes on the floor they are explored for their texture, unusual shapes and features before an old, vintage suitcase is introduced. The children are told that the suitcase is like a car and The Ogs use it to travel to children's favourite places. The children excitedly place The Ogs in and take them on an imaginary journey that ends by the large covered shape. The children remove the blanket to reveal a willow tipi large enough for them to climb inside. It has tiny furniture, cutlery made from recognisable household items and is immediately recognised as a home.

The children are handed a large book made from an old sheepskin rug with drawings of stick men inside which is the Og Diary. To ensure

(Continued)

(Continued)

Figure 9.1   Artist's impression of an Og hiding under clothes

the children have a reference point from which they can relate the time-scale, the storyteller/facilitator invites the children to consider contemporary, popular media representations that many children have access to (i.e. Animated Films that look at prehistoric times). Furthermore, using such a high visibility prop draws attention to a key part of the Og Toolkit and reinforces the idea that staff and children can use an Og Diary to record any interesting thoughts and marks that in time can lead to new stories, ideas and characters.

Turning old clothes into characters for learning

This phase of the workshop is expressed to the children as a simple Task:

'*New Ogs are coming to stay with you in the centre but we need to find them in the bags of clothes.*'

The children are given a large handmade Og Diary and invited to use the crayons and chalks to draw and make marks. The children scribble and express themselves with lines and colour and shapes. Children will be prompted to talk about colours and shapes that will be included in their final character design.

Prompt questions are prepared to stimulate the children's creativity. For example:

- Will your Og have any eyes?
- How will your Og move, does it have legs?

The drawings and thoughts are discussed as a group and with the support of staff decisions are taken about what will be made. The facilitator continually asks the children about shapes, choice of fabric and number of eyes etc. to keep them engaged. The children are introduced to an old manual sewing machine which they have noticed and once a shape is cut out of a piece of old clothing they turn the wheel by hand and watch their efforts produce stitches that will hold their Ogs together. Every effort is made to involve the children actively as a means of developing their sense of agency in the creation of the Ogs. Buttons and wool are used to give character to their creations and the resulting Ogs are introduced to the children and their reactions explored. It is a combination of the two pre-prepared stages that ensures the workshop has a lasting effect by encouraging each participant to feel part of this story and the development of other stories thereafter.

Once all participants had accessed workshop one and created their characters the children in each setting were brought together through co-constructive storytelling to support the collaborative nature of the workshop in bringing together children, service providers and the facilitator. This develops the overarching aims by supporting the children to develop the characters they have designed and create a world of their own making. The characters are brought to life allowing the children to construct meaning with creative freedom. The emphasis is very much on creativity as a collaborative experience.

Each setting's stories were created by the facilitator through the shared experiences of working together. The stories were made into books using photographs of the children in action as they expressed the story of their Ogs. The final stage for the children involved the centre

(Continued)

(Continued)

inviting them to make a home for the characters so they could be on display in the reception area. It was intended that all service users would then be able to access these resources and each would feel a sense of ownership and responsibility as they valued what had been created.

Case study 2: Involving adults in the child's creative work

In a response to the overarching aim of the facilitator (i.e. to develop a lifelong learning experience) and of the ICC Manager (to encourage all service users to engage in this creative process) parents of children attending the centre were invited to take part in a workshop.

The first attempt at running it through a formal written notice resulted in only one mother attending. This still proved a useful exercise as working one-to-one with the parent resulted in a co-created character that was designed as a helpful motivational tool. A character was designed to stimulate their child to walk without dawdling and complaining of it being too far to walk.

A second workshop was created spontaneously after a mother and toddler group session had finished. Parents were willing to stay on and partake in a workshop. Approximately seven mothers, one grandmother and younger siblings of the service users I had worked with took part. An explanation of the children's workshop was given and parents gave feedback on how their children had reacted to The Ogs.

The parents said that they had not become involved earlier due to their uncertainty about what was expected and a lack of confidence in their ability to be creative or sew. Constant references to lack of ability were overcome by showing the children's characters and sharing their own stories of how their children had engaged and interacted with The Ogs. Parents/guardians began to draw and cut and create characters. Younger children, not yet in Nursery, distracted themselves with materials and other toys available in the session, thus allowing the adults to fully explore the activity.

The adults commented on how surprised they were by their creations and how excited they were to get home and sort out their old clothes and engage with their children and their characters. All of the children had hands-on experience of tools and materials used in the creative play as a sensory exercise. There were opportunities for experiential learning when introduced to new tools and techniques

All children had the experience of working as a team to produce an outcome, i.e. taking recognisable, accessible materials to co-create a fabric character that will be shared and used by children and staff in their setting and taking turns.

The staff, parents and guardians were given the opportunity to be creative with the children. Importantly, the activities helped to break down barriers linked to their perceived lack of skill and ideas, so promoting the potential for creativity. Cost can also be prohibitive and the workshop showed ways in which everyday objects can be reused to create characters that stimulated the child's imagination. Therefore, the ability to be creative with easily available materials is demonstrated which can further undermine any fears of accessibility amongst parents, carers, etc.

Theory into practice

What is your motivation? If we are expecting to motivate the children we work with we can learn a lot from understanding why we chose certain activities to deliver to the class. As we explore our own motivation we become more aware of the motivation of others. The children's motivation may be very instinctive, spontaneous and primal depending on age and development. Our own motivation may be at times functional and at times altruistic. Our need to achieve goals may make it somewhat functional yet our inner desire to make a difference to the lives of others may make it more philanthropic. Both ends of this spectrum can encourage varying degrees of uncertainty but by identifying where you are on that spectrum can help you determine your boundaries as a creative practitioner.

What are you intending to achieve in your work? Are you striving to impart information through creative activities or are you intending to enhance and develop knowledge through creative activities? Depending on which end of this spectrum you feel comfortable with will determine where the emphasis lay with preparation. For example, if you are aiming to impart information the emphasis will need to be on how you engage the children in your chosen activity, whereas if you are aiming to allow more freedom to explore the learning and new interpretations to guide the exploration of learning, then the emphasis will be on how you manage the extraction of discourse among the group. Both approaches will need to have prepared a constructive way of recording how that learning has been indicated.

How could you develop the activity? Since the overall aim of the activity is promoting stimulating, safe, creativity there will always be other ways and practices that could have been used. Often it is the endlessness of the creative process that can be off-putting. There is no right and wrong way or an exact outcome but rather a series of experiences that will hold different values for the individual child, the practitioner and the group as a whole. Some thought needs to be given to each perspective and their potentials and limitations constructively considered. For example, did everyone have an opportunity to take part in the activity? Were there any highs and lows to the session? Did you notice when you had engaged all or most of the children and did you notice how long you had their attention? On the other hand, did you notice when the children had lost interest? In response to the answers to these questions you are in a better position to critically evaluate the activity

Key considerations when storytelling

What makes a good story? Below are some useful considerations to help develop and structure storytelling sessions:

- Emotional reaction – funny, sad, frightening, interesting, relaxing, energising.
- Audience – age, culture, language, length, timing, setting.
- Structure – stories need a start, a middle and an end. Consider the game of 'Consequences'.
- Introduce your character – name, favourite colour, likes, dislikes, where they live, special skills, best friend.
- Give your story a purpose – educational; a moral discussion; describing something such as a journey, place, person, behaviour, a key subject; impart information; a mystery; explore a question; provide an explanation; teach a new skill.
- Consider an opening line.

Duffy (2006) argues that creativity and imagination are vital in the Early Years and in fact throughout life. The prerequisites for stories that will capture the imagination of an Early Years audience centre themselves on key visual and structural criteria being met. For example, the structure and flow of the story will need to be digestible whilst also gaining the child's attention immediately. The length of the story will have been considered alongside a clear, simple, sentence formation to keep the listener involved and enable the characters and purpose to be revealed. The visual appearance of a book and the opportunities for reader and listener to interact with

Table 9.2 How the case studies link to the Foundation Phase and Foundation Stage

Foundation Phase	Foundation Stage	Case study 1	Case study 2
Personal and Social Development, Well-being and Cultural Diversity	Personal, Social and Emotional Development	Opportunity to work collaboratively, exploring, sharing and expressing differences and individuality	Developed confidence in creative ability. Appreciation of how creative play and storytelling can help with overcoming emotions such as anxiety and a lack of experience
Language, Literacy and Communication Skills	Communication and Language
Literacy	Using simple characters and storytelling to engage children in learning and develop confidence to speak through and voice opinions	Opportunity to experience the value of creative play to construct stories that can engage their children in learning
Welsh Language Development		The activity can be done through the medium of Welsh and bilingually	Opportunities to use Welsh vocabulary for role play
Mathematical Development	Mathematics	Opportunity to consider mathematical terms and number identification through storytelling and character development	
Knowledge and Understanding of the World	Understanding of the World	Opportunity to consider the world they live in as a home, a resource, as something to be shared with others and as something they are part of creating	Opportunity to consider the world they live in as a home, a resource, as something to be shared with others and as something they are part of creating
Physical Development	Physical development	Motor skills are developed through simple mark making and sensory awareness when accessing craft materials. Through active involvement in storytelling movement and physical self-expression are experienced	Creative craft encouraged fine motor skills to be developed and through actively developing their own storytelling, physical activity and self-expression are provoked
Creative Development	Expressive Arts and Design	Taking recognisable objects and disposable items and seeing their creative potential as something different and useful	Taking recognisable objects and disposable items and seeing their creative potential as something different and useful

a story will also enhance the experience. Furthermore, the purpose of a story will have been considered to ensure it has relevance and familiarity to the listener's world or, if introducing new phenomena, an opportunity for explanation and discussion is allowed for.

Such considerations provide a guide for practitioners when developing a story or when choosing a story. A story can start with a simple idea in the practitioner's or child's mind or may involve a published book but can end as a newly created tangible representation in the form of a new story that children have extended to allow them to play a fundamental part. Alternatively, children may use their own imagination to express the story using different materials and rather than the written word will use a series of pictures or creative objects.

In practice seeking to record the outcomes of storytelling and creative craft for soft skill development, such as use of language, self-expression, coordination and listening, can be challenging but is rarely overlooked by the active practitioner. Recording feedback from children's exposure to creative play and storytelling requires a qualitative approach that observes and records a child's emotional, cognitive and physical development.

Critical reflection on the case studies

Introducing the art of storytelling encourages creative thought, self-expression, respect for listening and helping thought processing by prompting discussion and language development. Creating diaries and characters develops children's fine motor skills, concentration, imagination, team and independent work. They can give children a voice and the Og stories complement most subjects in the Early Years frameworks and can be adapted for Foundation Stage, KS1 and KS2.

Statutory curricula in both England and Wales encourage children to be creative and imaginative to make learning more enjoyable and more effective.

Transitions and home–school links

Mindham (2010) asked the question is the provision for and appreciation of creativity to be extended beyond the Foundation Stage and should it be given more of a position in the key areas of numeracy and literacy? Due to the nature of the skills now being developed, transition may be less of an issue in this creative area as they can be integrated and developed across the curriculum at all levels. The two case studies focus on concepts and activities that can be engaged with across the primary age span.

The Foundation Stage has very clearly defined outcomes for Expressive Arts and Design. Before moving into Years 1 and 2, children have had experience of the following:

- Exploring and using media and materials: sing songs, make music and dance, and experiment with ways of changing them. Safely use and explore a variety of materials, tools and techniques, experimenting with colour, design, texture, form and function (as demonstrated in Case study 2).
- Being imaginative: children use what they have learnt about media and materials in original ways, thinking about uses and purposes. They represent their own ideas, thoughts and feelings through design and technology, art, music, dance, role-play and stories (as demonstrated in Case study 1).

In the Foundation Phase, there are six expected outcomes before the transition into Year 1 and 2. They broadly focus on:

- exploration and manipulation of resources and tools
- developing musical skills, e.g. making sounds; recognising music and moving to music; imitating actions, sounds and words; showing an awareness of some musical elements and expressing their ideas and moods such as happy or sad to playing simple tunes
- developing the use of lines and shapes to create symbols and images and assemble things that have meaning for them
- responding to open questions about their work and the work of others
- interpreting different stimuli such as music, words and pictures by moving in different ways, creating varied body shapes and changing direction
- performing simple action songs and nursery rhymes with others, broadly matching dynamics or other musical elements; developing singing skills in terms of tune, memory and rhythm

All of these outcomes can be built on throughout the Foundation Phase and in Years 1 and 2 of the National Curriculum in England. The important thing is to develop confidence and the willingness to engage in creative activities.

Questions for your practice

To summarise, the following key aspects are valuable to consider:

[1] Creativity should not be viewed in narrow terms, so think about how you could incorporate creativity in all aspects of the frameworks?
[2] Does creativity become 'watered down' as the child become older? If so, how do we maintain the curiosity, enthusiasm and lack of fear that we see in the early years?
[3] How could you adopt the principles in the case study into your own practice?

Summary

Craft (2003) talked about the relevance of using imagination, intelligences and self-expression to support children across the breadth of life's contexts. This chapter has focused on two practitioner experiences that show how we can effectively use creativity to develop confidence and unleash a wide range of positive experiences and relevant life skills.

Recommendations for further reading

Duffy, B. (2006) *Supporting Creativity and Imagination in the Early Years*. Maidenhead: Open University Press. The book uses real-life examples of young children's development and their growing competence to show the richness of their creativity and imagination. It contains very useful guidance on planning and assessing a child's progress.

McLellan, R., Galton, M., Stewart, S. and Page, C. (2012) *The Impact of Creative Partnerships on the Wellbeing of Children and Young People*. Newcastle: Creativity, Culture and Education. An excellent literature review focusing on the importance of creativity to well-being.

Ofsted (2012) *Learning: Creative Approaches that Raise Standards*. HMI 080266. Available at: www.creativitycultureeducation.org/wp-content/uploads/

learning-creative-approaches-that-raise-standards-250.pdf (accessed 26 August 2016). This survey evaluates how 44 schools used creative approaches to learning and challenges you to think about this in relation to your own practice.

Parry, B. (2010) 'Helping children tell the stories in their heads', in C. Bazalgette (ed.), *Teaching Media in Primary Schools*. London: Sage. pp. 89–101. The focus of the book is how media education enables children to become more fully literate for the digital age. It is an interesting and relevant book about the role of technology but also has a excellent chapter on children telling stories.

References

Craft, A. (2003) 'Creative thinking in the Early Years of education', *Early Years*, 23 (2): pp. 143–54.

DfE (Department for Education) (2014) *Statutory Framework for the Early Years Foundation Stage: Setting the standards for learning, development and care for children from birth to five*. London: DfE.

Duffy, B. (2006) *Supporting Creativity and Imagination in the Early Years*. Maidenhead: Open University Press.

Mellou, E. (1996) 'Can creativity be nurtured in young children?', *Early Child Development and Care*, 119: 119–30.

Mindham, C. (2010) 'Creativity and the young child', *Early Years*, 25 (1): 81–4.

Prentice, R. (2000) 'Creativity: a reaffirmation of its place in early childhood education', *Curriculum Journal*, 11 (2): 145–58.

Russ, S. W. (2003) 'Play and creativity: developmental issues', *Scandinavian Journal of Educational Research*, 47 (3): 291–303.

Welsh Government (2015) *Curriculum for Wales: Foundation Phase Framework (Revised 2015)*. Cardiff: Welsh Government.

INTO THE GREAT OUTDOORS: OPPORTUNITIES AND EXPERIENCES

Alyson Lewis and Rebecca Poole

Reading this chapter will help you to understand that learning outdoors is an important aspect of Early Years practice, particularly since the introduction in 2008 of the Early Years Foundation Stage (EYFS) in England, for 0–5-year-olds, and the Foundation Phase in Wales, for 3–7-year-olds. Far more emphasis is placed upon risk-taking, experiential learning and utilising the indoor *and* outdoor environment and seeing them as integrated, rather than using the outdoors as an add-on or a place where children let off steam (Bilton, 2010; Palaiologou, 2016; WAG, 2009). Children should not be deprived of the outdoor environment (Bilton, 2010), and the Welsh Assembly Government (WAG, 2008) advocate that free-flow access between the indoors *and* outdoors is beneficial to holistic development and health and well-being. However, Maynard and Waters (2007) report that practitioners are often working in school buildings that do not have easy, free-flow access to the outdoors and this makes it challenging. Knight (2013) reports that since the revised EYFS in 2012, the emphasis upon accessing the outdoors on a daily basis in England has been removed, but the message about the importance of learning outdoors has stayed the same.

We argue that practitioners play a crucial role in ensuring that children experience meaningful and worthwhile outdoor learning experiences, and we aim to demonstrate this through three case studies. According to Waite

(2011), in order for practitioners to value the potential of the outdoor environment they need to appreciate the principles of a playful pedagogy and have a sound knowledge of child development.

It is widely acknowledged that children's opportunities to play in natural outdoor spaces and to take risks are reducing (Bilton, 2010, 2012; Clements, 2004; Hope et al., 2007; Waters and Begley, 2007). Certain factors have been suggested to explain this decline, such as environmental changes, parental views and values and advanced technologies (Bilton, 2002; Edgington, 2003; Garrick, 2004; Harriman, 2006; Jenkinson, 2001; Knight, 2009; McClintic and Petty, 2015; Rickinson et al., 2004; Rivkin, 1995; Tovey, 2007; Waller, 2007). However, there have always been concerns about the decline in outdoor play for children. For example, commentators in the nineteenth century blamed early industrialisation, and in the twentieth century the radio and cinema were blamed. Most recently, digital technology and social media are responsible for the decline (Bishop and Curtis, 2001). Valentine et al. (2000) suggest there is a moral panic and adults quickly make assumptions about technology and how it contributes to children in negative ways. Despite what you feel about the decline or your general feeling towards outdoor play, it is imperative that settings provide quality outdoor learning experiences where children can take risks, be creative and develop knowledge and understanding of the world. We aim to show this through three case studies from an EYFS Reception class. Therefore, this chapter will enable you to learn about:

- how pioneers have contributed to contemporary thinking about the outdoors
- the concept of affordance and how this relates to the outdoor space
- the benefits of children learning outdoors and the importance of Forest School
- the role of the adult in promoting risky-play and some of the challenges faced by practitioners in facilitating learning outdoors

Key words

risky-play, Forest School, development, affordance, environment, playful pedagogy, heuristic play

Theoretical perspectives

Historical perspectives

Many pioneers around the eighteenth and nineteenth century contributed to promoting Early Childhood Education and Care (ECEC) at a time of war, deprivation and inequality. Rousseau (1712–1778), Pestalozzi (1746–1827) and Owen (1771–1858) frequently referred to 'garden' activities to explain good practice. They advocated that the outdoors was a place for educational reform (Joyce, 2012), and was seen as having health benefits for children (Bilton, 2010). For example, McMillan focused her work on utilising the outdoor space for improving health and well-being at a time, in 1911, when disease, infection and health problems were widespread (Tovey, 2007; Wood and Attfield, 2005). However, Montessori (1869–1952) was concerned more with the scientific aspect of nature and viewed the outdoors as a place for growing plants and vegetables. She instigated the idea of free-flow access and encouraged children to take on purposeful roles to understand their moral responsibilities (Tovey, 2007).

Isaacs (1885–1948) considered the outdoors as a place where children could be inspired and enthused and have the freedom to think and move. Similarly, Froebel (1982–1852) strongly believed the outdoors provided children with opportunities to find a sense of belonging in the natural world and a place where they could find peace (Wood and Attfield, 2005). But Isaacs was better known for allowing children to dissect dead animals and encouraging curiosity and exploration (Tovey, 2007). Furthermore, Isaacs' work has helped us understand how first-hand outdoor learning experiences promote cognitive development (Garrick, 2004; Wood and Attfield, 2005). There is evidence to suggest that children who experience regular opportunities outdoors show improved academic success and emotional, social and physical well-being, but most of the research relates to school-age children rather than the under-fives (Merewether, 2015). Despite this, numerous studies that focus on children's environments report that children have a preference for playing outdoors (Merewether, 2015).

Experiencing the outdoors

The following factors draw children to the outdoors, for example its awe and wonder, more open space and more freedom, and positive attitudes from educators, more choice with equipment, as well as open-ended resources that facilitate challenge and encourage discovery (Bilton, 2010; Huggins and Wickett, 2011; Merewether, 2015; Ouvry, 2003; Ryder-Richardson, 2006;

Tovey, 2007; Waite and Pratt, 2011; Waller, 2011). Moreover, children have a preference for creative agency and relationships, but these are not unique to the outdoors. These factors highlight the importance of Vygotsky's and Bruner's thinking in Early Years settings that focus on the social aspect of learning and a sense of belonging (Merewether, 2015). The 'mud kitchen' case study below aims to show how children enact creative agency. Opportunities for pretend play are sometimes limited due to curriculum demands, but children construct knowledge through pretend play; and there are endless opportunities for children to do this outdoors (Merewether, 2015). The outdoors also provides numerous opportunities for children to develop the 'enactive' mode of learning (Bruner, 1971). This mode of learning is characterised by doing and actions (Bruner, 1971).

The theory of *affordance* (i.e. possibilities) (Gibson, 1979; Greeno, 1994) is significant when discussing what the outdoor space offers children, and the concept is discussed at length by various researchers, such as Fjørtoft (2001), Barab and Roth (2006) to name but a few. More recently, Mawson (2014) discusses the range of affordances provided by the natural, wild-woods environment. Kytta (2002; cited in Niklasson and Sandberg, 2010) suggests there are four different levels of affordances:

[1] Potential
[2] Perceived
[3] Utilised
[4] Shaped

The mud kitchen case study draws upon some of these levels in more detail.

The Researching Effective Pedagogy in the Early Years (REPEY) project found that the majority of practitioners viewed 'physical development' as the main affordance (Siraj-Blatchford et al., 2002) and much of the literature often focuses on physical development and movement (Bilton, 2002; Clements, 2004). However, Ouvry (2003) and Tovey (2007) argue that every Area of Learning in the curriculum can be developed and enhanced outside, as well as promoting general health and well-being (Elliott, 2010). In other words, there are many affordances, however the benefits linked to outdoor play and the pedagogical practices are under-researched (Joyce, 2012; Muñoz, 2009).

Obesity in young children is a growing concern along with the inactive lifestyle to which some children are accustomed, so it is vital that settings make full use of their outdoor environment to help combat such an issue (Brussoni et al., 2012; Edgington, 2003). The Forest School approach which is gaining momentum in the UK is considered a useful way to help reduce child obesity, as well as improve behaviour, social skills and language development (Knight, 2013). Maynard (2007a) suggests there is more interest in Forest School due to a decline in outdoor play.

Forest School pedagogy

Forest School originated in Denmark and was first developed in the UK in 1993 (Knight, 2013; Maynard, 2007a). Sessions are usually held regularly in nearby woodland and led by an adult who had undertaken Forest School training. The area is made as safe as is reasonably possible (Knight, 2013). Knight (2013) highlights that children are trusted as competent and able beings and learning is play-based and child-led. Taking risks is central to Forest School and the high practitioner ratio of adults to children facilitates risky activities, such as building fires (Waters and Begley, 2007). Beames (2013) concurs that risky and adventurous play should not be exclusive to Forest School but should be happening in and around the school grounds and nearby neighbourhoods as part of heuristic play.

Research about Forest School is growing and sceptics are keen to know more about the benefits. Passy and Waite (2011) suggest that most of the research conducted about Forest School is carried out by enthusiasts, which raises questions about subjectivity. Sometimes the benefits in relation to self-esteem are over-emphasised and environmental education is under-emphasised (Maynard, 2007b). Generally, the following positive outcomes are associated with Forest School:

- increased confidence
- improved social skills and language and communication skills
- improved motivation and sustained concentration
- improved physical strength and ability
- an increase in knowledge and understanding of the world
- some evidence of the ripple effect, where children ask to go outdoors more at the weekends and holidays (Knight, 2013; Ridgers et al., 2012).

For children to truly benefit from the great outdoors they need adults who genuinely believe in its potential (Bilton, 2010; Waller, 2011). McMillan (1919: 81; cited in Bilton, 2010) once stated that teachers can either help or hinder children's successes. Bilton (2010) agrees, and states that practitioners are crucial in helping children to progress and develop.

The role of the adult

Providing quality outdoor experiences

Quality outdoor experiences rest with the practitioners, who are an essential resource (Bilton, 2010; Tovey, 2007; White, 2011) and they should aim to develop the following qualities in children, such as playfulness, enthusiasm and curiosity (Clements, 2004). The way practitioners perceive children and the curriculum, determines the provision, care and pedagogy of a setting (Dahlberg et al., 1999). According to Joyce (2012: 102), aspects of practice such as pedagogy and sustained shared thinking need to be at the forefront of practice. Huggins and Wickett (2011) argue that a shared pedagogy needs to be established for the outdoor environment.

For learning to take place outside, settings must have clear, focused aims and well-planned activities (Edgington, 2003; Ouvry, 2003). Bilton (2002, 2010) and Brown et al. (2009) argue that it is unacceptable to have planning for indoor provision and not to have it for outdoor provision. Tovey (2007) suggests that planning and adult-led tasks are often required for facilitating learning outdoors. Ouvry (2003) explains that the outdoor environment is best utilised when practitioners have a confident and secure understanding of their role in developing learning. Huggins and Wickett (2011) report that children are more likely to learn effectively outdoors when practitioners have a sound knowledge of child development.

In 2006, Waite and Rea (cited in Waite, 2011) found that practitioners demonstrated a lack of understanding and an awareness of the outdoor environment in Welsh schools. Furthermore, in 2011, Estyn (the Education and Training Inspectorate in Wales) reported that settings and local authorities need to provide training for all staff so they become knowledgeable and confident about the benefits of outdoor learning. They further report that senior members of staff are often poorly trained in improving the outdoor provision. In 2011, Estyn (2011) evaluated the outdoor learning in the Foundation Phase and found that in comparison to the indoors, teachers tend to carry out assessment of learning less well in the outdoors. Also, teachers are more unlikely to track children's progress when they engage with learning

(Continued)

(Continued)

outside. Despite some of these weaknesses, Estyn (2011) found that strong leadership and vision helps to overcome some of the challenges faced by practitioners.

In 2015, the Welsh Government published their findings from a three-year independent evaluation of the Foundation Phase, and found that practitioners rarely used the outdoor learning environment to extend children's learning (Taylor et al., 2015). The researchers also found that teaching assistants were observed outside more often than a teacher. Year 1 children who participated in walking tours said they rarely did any learning outside (Taylor et al., 2015). In 2011, Ofsted (2011) found that in many settings in England, the outdoor learning opportunities were very poor compared with the indoor opportunities on offer for children. The EYFS refers to the 'enabling environment' as one of its overarching principles, however the curriculum framework is not explicit about whether this is both the indoors and the outdoors.

Barriers and challenges

Curriculum demands have possibly hindered the time children play outside in the school day (Bilton, 2010; Ernst, 2014). Also, parents and practitioners often blame poor weather for children getting colds, yet research suggests that getting colds is to do with the cold virus that lives in us, not to do with 'perceived' cold viruses that 'live' in the fresh air (Bilton, 2010). Therefore, it is important that children wear appropriate clothing and are encouraged to look after their health. There is a famous Nordic saying that, 'there is no such thing as bad weather, only bad clothing' (Joyce, 2012)! Other factors that could hinder children's experiences outdoors are suggested by Alderson (2008), who states that keeping children safe and protecting them actually restricts them from many opportunities to learn and discover. Moreover, it restricts them from assessing risk, making their own decisions and building confidence in managing situations (Stephenson, 2003; Waite, 2011).

Another factor that could prevent children from experiencing the outdoors is the reluctance of practitioners (Bilton, 2010). Moyles (2001) suggests that staff should allocate time to discuss issues that evoke their thoughts and feelings about children playing outdoors, but many settings do not allocate time to reflect in general (MacNaughton, 2005). Tovey (2007) suggests that staff need to be prepared to confront their perceptions about children's play. However, in order to achieve this, Moyles (2001)

suggests that practitioners need to demonstrate very high levels of professional capacity and self-confidence, which are often lacking in many female
early childhood professionals. When professionals attempt to confront their
perceptions about outdoor play there always tend to be disagreements, a
lack of commitment and vision, and uncertainty (Ouvry, 2003).

Pedagogical approaches

The role of the adult is important when developing and using the outdoor
space. According to Stephenson (2002), there are usually two different
types of approaches adopted by practitioners: 'monitorial' and 'interactive'.
The monitorial approach is more supervisory in nature, whereas the interactive approach is more collaborative and associated with more affordances.
However, practitioners have a tendency to assign play areas and monitor
what children do (Ward, 1990), and according to Casey (2007), children are
very good at utilising play equipment correctly to please adults, but very
quickly they avert to using equipment for their own intentions. When children transform their outdoor play space in a way that suits them, it indicates
that they are truly connected with it (Casey, 2007). However, there runs the
risk of children's mastery motivation and curiosity being eliminated when
adults place too much control on children and limit their amount of choice
(Maynard, 2007b). Practitioners should aim to adopt a socio-constructionist
approach to working in the outdoors. This is where the time is negotiated
with children who are given the opportunity to decide whether they continue to rest, work or play (MacNaughton, 2003). Huggins and Wickett
(2011) argue that for children to engage in sustained shared thinking, they
need to experience extended periods of uninterrupted time.

Clements (2004) states that when children choose their agenda this leads
to fulfilment and motivation, which is one of the most valuable outdoor
experiences children can have. Moore (1986) suggests that making decisions about resources and allocating money to equipment is a waste of
time if practitioners have not considered what the children enjoy doing and
where they play. Practitioners should aim to seek children's views on what
should change or stay the same (Casey, 2007) and respect what they have
to say (Lansdown, 1995; Thomas, 2001) as it can be enlightening and helpful (Nutbrown and Hannon, 2003). Tovey (2007) suggests that practitioners
should understand and acknowledge that children are experts in their own
lives and should be listened to.

In the last twenty years there has been a considerable amount of research
conducted in the field of Early Years, but very little has focused on outdoor
learning and the young child's perspective (Clements, 2004; Garrick, 2004;

Rickinson et al., 2004; Waller, 2006). Greig et al. (2007: 96) argue that genuine listening to children is a neglected area in early childhood research. The outdoor space should represent the children's suggestions (Tovey, 2007) because too much of children's time and space is currently arranged by adults (Alderson, 2008). It is only in the past ten years or so that research *with* children has gradually gained momentum. One reason for this is the new sociology of childhood perspective, which views children as social actors, strong, capable, competent beings, skilful communicators and meaning-makers (Clark and Moss, 2005; Merewether, 2015).

Case studies

Case study 1: Taking a risk

On deciding to go outside, James made his way towards the wooden gazebo and climbed onto the surrounding ledge, which is about one metre high, and jumped onto the grass below (see Figure 10.1).

Figure 10.1 James jumping one metre from the ground with two other children observing

Figure 10.2   Sarah on the far left joining in

Two other children were observing James nearby whom then followed by jumping onto the grass. Soon after, Sarah started to join in, firstly by sitting on the surrounding ledge and jumping onto the grass from a sitting position (see Figure 10.2).

Very soon after jumping from a sitting position, Sarah was encouraged by the boys to stand on the surrounding ledge to jump (see Figure 10.3). James said: *'I'll jump with you.'*

James and Sarah spent around 30 minutes repeatedly climbing the gazebo and jumping off and appeared to be setting themselves new challenges. Sarah said: *'I will say go, then you can jump.'* James replied: *'Okay, my turn.'* James jumped and said: *'That was super-fast!'* Sarah and James took it in turns to jump and waited until it was safe to do so. James noticed another child watching them and he turned to her and said: *'Do you want a go? I can help you.'* She shook her head, and James turned to Sarah and said: *'She doesn't fancy it.'*

Sarah continued to jump and each time she tried to make the jump more exciting and adventurous by standing as tall as she could and

(Continued)

(Continued)

Figure 10.3   Sarah jumping from a standing position

pushing off with her feet saying: *'Imagine you jump right into the sky!'* Once she landed, she said: *'Ow, I've broken my leg. No I'm only joking, I'm just kidding.'* James said after a particularly high jump: *'That didn't hurt me, just my eyes.'*

Case study 2: Mud kitchen

Luke replied to an adult: *'We're collecting prickles for our potion; the potion will kill the baddies.'* John suggested: *'Let's make a stinging potion.'* The boys ventured towards the mud kitchen and found a large saucepan for their potion and the following dialogue took place:

John said:	*It's really heavy, I need some help to lift it.*
Luke said:	*We are making a bad potion, I'll mix it.*
Albert added:	*I'm going to make the baddest potion!*
Luke replied:	*I'm going to make the horriblest potion!*
James poured water from a bottle into the pan of mixed leaves and thorns and said:	*Urgh! That was grey water.*

John said:	*Oh that's definitely disgusting, I'm putting it in. You guys come and whisk it.*
James added:	*That smells stinky!*
John said:	*Add some stones.*
James asked:	*Who wants some water?*
Luke replied:	*Me!*
James said:	*We are sharing it.*
John said:	*I'm putting a bad flavour in.*
Albert added:	*Yes, this is going to smell.*

John picked up a rusty, battered sieve and said, *Time to grate.*

James asked his peers:	*Where is the oven?*
Luke replied:	*Over there!* [pointing under the table]
James added:	*We will need some fire, come on rub some sticks together, we can make a fire, rub sticks.*
Luke found a long stick and broke it in half and said:	*I've got two sticks now, I can do that, get rubbing.*
Another child came along and asked:	*What are you making?*
John replied:	*We are making a stinky potion for the baddies.*
James explained:	*We are getting mud from under that tree but we need water to get the mud out, it's too hard.*
John added:	*Yes we need water so we can dig down.*
James brought the water container over to the patch of dry mud under the oak tree, he explained:	*There is sand in here, we need sand to mix the mud but I can't get it out. If we tip it upside down we can get the sand out. You need to pat it.*

The boys fetched wooden spoons and spatulas from the mud kitchen and started hitting the plastic water container. Luke used a ball on a rope to hit the container.

James said:	*No, stop! You can't use that it will break. No, you are not allowed to use that, the ball might, you might hurt yourself.*

(Continued)

(Continued)

A second later Luke swung the ball towards his head on purpose and said:

Ow! That hurt my head.

James explained:

You have to tap it [the water container] then the sand will come out. Let's lift it. I want to see if any sand camed out.

The boys squealed with delight and cheered in unison as a mountain of sand was deposited on the dry ground.

The boys returned to their potions and removed them from the pots and pans using large tweezers. John started to hit his pan with his wooden spoon and the other boys copied. *'They can be drums,'* he said. After five minutes of playing the drums, James suggested they became a marching band and stood up with his pan and spatula and said: *'Let's march with our drums,'* and off they went around the field (see Figure 10.4).

Figure 10.4   Children using the resources as drums

Theory into practice

In this section we discuss the two case studies from the EYFS Reception class and show you how they link with the theory of affordance. The first case study demonstrates how children make their own decisions about risk and support one another, whilst the second case study demonstrates children's creative agency. Both case studies demonstrate the importance of learning in a social context, which are ideas argued by Vygotsky and Bruner (Merewether, 2015). They also highlight the affordances offered to children (Kytta, 2002; cited in Niklasson and Sandberg, 2010). Both case studies include examples of the enactive mode of learning (Bruner, 1971). This is where children engage in active, experiential, physical experiences.

Taking a risk

The first case study shows how a 4-year-old child called James, who is often timid and reserved, initiated a risky experience outdoors. This highlights the importance of providing daily outdoor experiences that allow children to develop holistically. Without the outdoor experience, developing confidence and building relationships with others might become more difficult for James. This case study demonstrates his ability to encourage and support other children, particularly Sarah. James is acting out the support of the knowledgeable other and helping his peers within their Zone of Proximal Development (ZPD). Fisher (2013) describes Vygotsky's ZPD as the gap between what children can accomplish alone, and what they can go on to achieve with the help of a more able other. In this case, the more able other is another child and we argue that other children are invaluable in helping children grow in emotional and physical strength.

James and Sarah constantly checked and talked about the risk and Knight (2011) asserts that children need to encounter risk during development. Furthermore, Moss and Petrie (2002) concur that children are experts in the decisions they make, and are capable of making their own judgements about risk, which is shown by James and Sarah in this case study.

Finally, this case study evidences the four levels of affordances particularly offered to Sarah:

[1] the 'potential' opportunities of the gazebo being used as a risky platform for jumping
[2] the 'perceived' risk of jumping and needing the support of others to help her in this process
[3] the 'utilised' risky space of having the confidence to jump from a high level and
[4] the 'shaped' and extended learning experience that occurred between Sarah and James.

This case study also shows that Sarah was provided with a rich opportunity to overcome fear but with the help of her friend James. Links to the curriculum include personal, social and emotional development as well as physical development. The children clearly used the gazebo for a different purpose and Casey (2007) suggests that when children are able to decide on how to use outdoor equipment they truly become connected with it. We would argue that this case study is a rich enactive mode of learning (Bruner, 1971) where the children are provided with endless opportunities to move freely.

Mud kitchen

The dialogue for this case study took place between a group of 4-to-5-year-olds who decided to go outdoors due to their free-flow provision, and after a period of superhero role play, they started to collect different types of leaves where their play extended into the mud kitchen. The affordances in the dialogue show how the mud kitchen prompted the children's imagination and creativity, and provided them with a sensory experience and opportunities to share, take turns and listen to each other to name but a few (Hammond, 2007; Williams-Siegfredson, 2005). It is an example of Affordance 3, called 'utilised' (Kytta; 2002, cited in Niklasson and Sandberg, 2010). The children utilised the resources and their ideas as well as utilising their physical strength. In addition, the children demonstrated their ability to communicate early scientific concepts when they were making the potion. For example, James explained to his peers that the mud was very hard and the water would help to get it out from the ground. Strong links can be made here to the area of learning 'Understanding the World' where children make observations and talk about changes to materials (Early Education, 2012). The children were continuously solving problems throughout the entire time of making their potion.

This case study also shows how they confidently and creatively enact pretend play. The mud kitchen dialogue shows how children's physical development is enhanced and concludes with a music focus, which is an example of Affordance 4 called 'shaped' (Kytta; 2002, cited in Niklasson and Sandberg, 2010). The resources available to the children in the mud kitchen and the children's ability to use them creatively also allow them to begin exploring sound, rhythm and early music-making concepts; an important area of learning within the curriculum. This case study highlights the learning opportunities afforded to children by providing them with open-ended resources that facilitate challenge and encourage discovery. Bruner's (1971) concept of the enactive mode of learning was evidenced throughout, from the moment the children starting collecting leaves to using the instruments. The children were free to construct the learning experience.

The role of the adult

Collectively, the case studies show how practitioners are an essential resource in promoting and extending learning outdoors (Bilton, 2010; Tovey, 2007; White, 2011). However, the adult's input in both case studies was very minimal, which raises the point about the importance of observation. In the risk-taking case study, adults were flexible and adaptable in allowing the children to explore the gazebo and manage their own risks. They did not interfere and provided minimal, subtle intervention (Knight, 2011). Adams (2001) warns that if practitioners constantly manage the risk decisions, children's ability to make decisions about risk is constrained. The children quickly decided to use the gazebo as a climbing structure, which probably was not the original intention of the adults (Casey, 2007), but this highlights how comfortable and at ease the adults were with the new use of the gazebo. More importantly, the adults saw beyond the original intention of the gazebo and were interested in the affordances offered to children. The adults were not being monitorial in any way or controlling the situation (Stephenson, 2002).

In the mud kitchen case study the adults initially interacted by showing an interest in what they were doing, then they observed the children to see how they were utilising their space and respected what they saw (Jenkinson, 2001). Practitioners should be regularly reviewing the outdoor play space to gain a feeling for its success and observing the range of play types, the most and least favourite play resources or equipment, and the way in which children change their outdoor play space (Casey, 2007). The mud kitchen case study also shows how the children's play was uninterrupted and they were given autonomy to plan their play, which is a concept closely associated with the work of Frobel back in the nineteenth century (Tovey, 2007). The adults encouraged the children to develop the play at their own pace, allowing them to become truly engaged, therefore, sustaining their concentration (Huggins and Wickett, 2011).

Transitions and home–school links

The EYFP in Wales advocates free-flow access to the outdoors for 3–7-year-olds, therefore children are more than likely going to experience the transition to Year 3 in Key Stage 2 from daily outdoor provision in the

(Continued)

(Continued)

Early Years to weekly planned Physical Education (PE) lessons. In England, children in the EYFS may experience a similar transition but instead at the age of 5 in Key Stage 1 rather than at the age of 7. Therefore, we suggest that children should be provided with a range of learning experiences and opportunities and this should include being outdoors for children of all ages. It should be remembered that every subject area of a curriculum can be delivered and promoted outdoors (Ouvry, 2003; Tovey, 2007). The learning opportunities are endless when children are 'permitted' to explore the outdoors.

Children will develop their first experiences of the outdoors at home, and this may be a positive or negative experience. Some children may have had more risky play experiences, some may have had more 'messy, muddy' type experiences and some may have been protected and sheltered from the outdoors. Therefore, it is important for practitioners to acknowledge this. In terms of the gazebo risky-play case study and the way in which the children connected with it, practitioners may need to explain to parents/carers the important learning opportunities that were taking place – particularly if children start using outdoor equipment at home for their purpose and benefit which is different to its conventional use. Establishing a shared outdoor pedagogy (Huggins and Wickett, 2011) is important, and this should include home–school partnerships. Practitioners should be able to provide a rationale for risky-play activities and be confident to address some of the parental concerns that might arise, particularly about Forest School pedagogy.

Questions for your practice

[1] How could you develop your outdoor space so that it caters for children's holistic development and risky-play?
[2] How often do you consult the children in your setting about what they think about their outdoor environment?
[3] What kind of practitioner are you when you work with children outdoors: a supervisor, a worrier, or someone who observes, listens and interacts?

Summary

This chapter has summarised how pioneers have contributed to contemporary thinking about the outdoors, and briefly explained some of the factors that draw children towards the outdoors. The theory of affordance was drawn upon to discuss the benefits of Forest School and the outdoor environment more generally. 'Affordances' were further explored in two case studies. Evidence about current practice in England and Wales generally shows that practitioners need to improve the way they use the outdoor environment. Various challenges that practitioners face in ensuring children receive quality outdoor experiences were discussed, and listening to children's perspectives about their outdoor play space, and regarding them as experts in their experiences was suggested as a way forward in research and practice. The case studies demonstrated that the adults, the children themselves and the type of equipment available are some of the most important resources in ensuring quality outdoor experiences.

Recommendations for further reading

O'Brien, E. and Murray, R. (2006) *A Marvellous Opportunity for Children to Learn: A Participatory Evaluation of Forest School in England and Wales*. Surrey: Forest Research. www.forestry.gov.uk/pdf/fr0112forest-schoolsreport.pdf/$FILE/fr0112forestschoolsreport.pdf. This is a useful evaluative report about the impact of Forest School in England and Wales. It is also useful for those interested in adopting a 'participatory action-research' approach.

Outdoor Learning Wales. www.outdoorlearningwales.org/home This website provides information about a national network and is useful for those interested in sustainable management of natural resources.

White, J. (2013) *Playing and Learning Outdoors: Making Provision for High Quality Experiences in the Outdoor Environment with Children 3–7*. Abingdon: Routledge. This book provides practitioners with helpful advice and support about making the most of their outdoor space.

References

Adams, J. (2001) *Risk*. London: Routledge.

Alderson, P. (2008) *Young Children's Rights: Exploring Beliefs, Principles and Practice*, 2nd edn. London: Jessica Kingsley Publications.

Barab, S. and Roth, W. (2006) 'Curriculum-based ecosystems: Supporting knowing from an ecological perspective', *Educational Researcher*, 35 (5): 3–13.

Beames, S. (2013) 'Book Reviews: Risk and adventure in early years outdoor play, by Sara Knight', *Educational Review*, 65 (4): 502–15.

Bilton, H. (2002) *Outdoor Play in the Early Years: Management and Innovation*. London: David Fulton Publishers.

Bilton, H. (2010) *Outdoor Learning in the Early Years: Management and Innovation*, 3rd edn. London: David Fulton Publishers.

Bilton, H (2012) 'The type and frequency of interactions that occur between staff and children outside in Early Years Foundation Stage settings during a fixed playtime period when there are tricycles available', *European Early Childhood Education Research Journal*, 20 (3): 403–21.

Bishop, J.C. and Curtis, M. (2001) *Play Today in the Primary School Playground*. London: Open University Press.

Brown, W. H., Pfeiffer, K. A., McIver, K. L., Dowda, M., Addy, L. and Pate, R. R. (2009) 'Social and environmental factors associated with pre-schoolers' non-sedentary physical activity', *Child Development*, 80 (1): 45–58.

Bruner, J. S. (1971) *The Relevance of Education*. New York: Norton.

Brussoni, M., Olsen, L. L., Pike, I. and Sleet, D. A. (2012) 'Risky play and children's safety: Balancing priorities for optimal child development', *International Journal of Environmental Research and Public Health*, 9 (1): 3134–48.

Casey, T. (2007) *Environments for Outdoor Play: A Practical Guide to Making Space for Children*. London: Paul Chapman Publishing.

Clark, A. and Moss, P. (2005) *Spaces to Play: More Listening to Young Children using the Mosaic Approach*. London: National Children's Bureau.

Clements, R. (2004) 'An investigation of the status of outdoor play', *Contemporary Issues in Early Childhood*, 5 (1): 68–80.

Dahlberg, D., Moss, P. and Pence, A. (1999) *Beyond Quality in Early Childhood Education and Care: Postmodern Perspectives*. London: RoutledgeFalmer.

Early Education (2012) *Development Matters in the Early Years Foundation Stage*. [Online] Available from: www.foundationyears.org.uk/files/2012/03/Development-Matters-FINAL-PRINT-AMENDED (accessed 18 August 2016).

Edgington, M. (2003) *The Great Outdoors: Developing Children's Learning through Outdoor Provision*, 2nd edn. London: The British Association for Early Childhood Education.

Elliott, S. (2010) 'Children in the natural world', in J. Davis (ed.), *Young Children and the Environment: Early Education for Sustainability*. Melbourne: Cambridge University Press.

Ernst, J. (2014) 'Early childhood educators' use of natural outdoor settings as learning environments: an exploratory study of beliefs, practices, and barriers', *Environmental Education Research*, 20 (6): 735–52.

Estyn (2011) *Outdoor Learning: An Evaluation of Learning in the Outdoors for Children under 5 in the Foundation Phase*. Cardiff: Estyn.

Fisher, J. (2013) *Starting from the Child*, 4th edn. Maidenhead: Open University Press.

Fjørtoft, I. (2001) 'The natural environment as a playground for children: The impact of outdoor play activities in pre-primary school children', *Early Childhood Education Journal*, 29 (2): 111–17.

Garrick, R. (2004) *Playing Outdoors in the Early Years*. London: Continuum International Publishing Group.

Gibson, J. (1979) *The Ecological Approach to Visual Perception*. Boston, MA: Houghton–Mifflin.

Greeno, J. G. (1994) 'Gibson's affordances', *Psychological Review*, 101 (2): 336–42.

Greig, A., Taylor, J. and MacKay, T. (2007) *Researching with Children*, 2nd edn. London: Sage.

Hammond, S. (2007) 'Taking the inside out', in R. Austin (ed.), *Letting the Outside In: Developing Teaching and Learning Beyond the Early Years Classroom*. Staffordshire: Trentham Books.

Harriman, H. (2006) *The Outdoor Classroom: A Place to Learn*. Wiltshire: A Corner to Learn Ltd.

Hope, G., Austin, R., Dismore, H. and Hammond, S. (2007) 'Wild woods or urban jungle: Playing it safe or freedom to roam', *Education 3–13*, 35 (4): 321–32.

Huggins, V. and Wickett, K. (2011) 'Crawling and toddling in the outdoors: Very young children's learning', in S. Waite (ed.), *Children Learning Outside the Classroom*. London: Sage.

Jenkinson, S. (2001) *The Genius of Play: Celebrating the Spirit of Childhood*. Gloucestershire: Hawthorn Press.

Joyce, R. (2012) *Outdoor Learning Past and Present*. Maidenhead: Open University Press.

Knight, S. (2009) *Forest Schools and Outdoor Learning in the Early Years*. London: Sage.

Knight, S. (2011) *Risk and Adventure in Early Years Outdoor Play: Learning from Forest Schools*. London: Sage.

Knight, S. (2013) *Forest School and Outdoor Learning in the Early Years*, 2nd edn. London: Sage.

Lansdown, G. (1995) 'The Children's Rights Development Unit', in B. Franklin (ed.), *The Handbook of Children's Rights: Comparative Policy and Practice*. London: Routledge.

MacNaughton, G. (2003) *Shaping Early Childhood: Learners, Curriculum and Contexts*. Maidenhead: Open University Press.

MacNaughton, G. (2005) *Doing Foucault in Early Childhood Studies: Applying Poststructural Ideas*. London: Routledge.

Mawson, W. (2014) 'Experiencing the "wild woods": The impact of pedagogy on children's experience of a natural environment', *European Early Childhood Education Research Journal*, 22 (4): 513–24.

Maynard, T. (2007a) 'Making the best of what you've got: Adopting and adapting a Forest School approach', in R. Austin (ed.), *Letting the Outside In: Developing Teaching and Learning Beyond the Early Years Classroom*. Staffordshire: Trentham Books.

Maynard, T. (2007b) 'Forest Schools in Great Britain: An initial exploration', *Contemporary Issues in Early Childhood*, 8 (4): 320–31.

Maynard, T. and Waters, J. (2007) 'Learning in the outdoor environment: A missed opportunity?', *Early Years: An International Research Journal*, 27 (3): 225–65.

McClintic, S. and Petty, K. (2015) 'Exploring early childhood teachers' beliefs and practices about preschool outdoor play: A qualitative study', *Journal of Early Childhood Teacher Education*, 36 (1): 24–43.

Merewether, J. (2015) 'Young children's perspectives of outdoor learning spaces: What matters?', *Australasian Journal of Early Childhood*, 40 (1): 99–108.

Moore, R. C. (1986) *Childhood's Domain: Play and Place in Child Development*. London: Croom Helm.

Moss, P. and Petrie, P. (2002) *From Children's Services to Children's Spaces: Public Policy, Children and Childhood*. London: RoutledgeFalmer.

Moyles, J. (2001) 'Passion, paradox and professionalism in Early Years education', *Early Years*, 21 (2): 81–95.

Muñoz, S. (2009) *Children in the Outdoors: A Literature Review*. Forres: Sustainable Development Research Centre.

Niklasson, L. and Sandberg. A. (2010) 'Children and the outdoor environment', *European Early Childhood Education Research Journal*, 18: 485–96.

Nutbrown, C. and Hannon, P. (2003) 'Children's perspectives on family literacy: Methodological issues, findings and implications for practice', *Journal of Early Childhood Literacy*, 3 (2): 115–45.

Ofsted (2011) *The Impact of the Early Years Foundation Stage*. No.100231. London: Ofsted.

Ouvry, M. (2003) *Exercising Muscles and Minds: Outdoor Play and the Early Years Curriculum*. London: National Children's Bureau.

Palaiologou, I. (2016) *The Early Years Foundation Stage*, 3rd edn. London: Sage.

Passy, R. and Waite, S. (2011) 'School gardens and Forest Schools', in S. Waite (ed.), *Children Learning Outside the Classroom*. London: Sage.

Rickinson, M., Dillon, J., Teamey, K., Morris, M., Young Choi, M., Saunders, D. and Benefield, P. (2004) *A Review of Research on Outdoor Learning*. London: Field Studies Council.

Ridgers, N., Knowles, Z. and Sayers, J. (2012) 'Encouraging play in the natural environment: A child-focused case study of Forest School', *Children's Geographies*, 10 (1): 49–65.

Rivkin, M. (1995) *The Great Outdoors: Restoring Children's Right to Play Outside*. Washington: National Association for the Education of Young Children.

Ryder-Richardson, G. (2006) *Creating a Space to Grow: Developing Your Outdoor Learning Environment*. London: David Fulton Publishers.

Siraj-Blatchford, I., Sylva, K., Muttock, S., Gilden, R. and Bell, D. (2002) *Researching Effective Pedagogy in the Early Years*. London: Department for Education and Skills.

Stephenson, A. (2002) 'Opening up the outdoors: Exploring the relationship between the indoor and outdoor environments of a centre', *European Early Childhood Education Research Journal*, 10: 29–38.

Stephenson, A. (2003) 'Physical risk-taking: Dangerous or endangered?', *Early Years*, 23 (1): 35–43.

Taylor, C., Rhys, M., Waldron, S., Davies, R., Power, S., Maynard, T., Moore, L., Blackaby, D. and Plewis, I. (2015) *Evaluating the Foundation Phase: Final Report*. Cardiff: Welsh Government.

Thomas, N. (2001) 'Listening to children', in P. Foley, J. Roche and S. Tucker (eds), *Children in Society: Contemporary Theory, Policy and Practice*. Basingstoke: Palgrave.

Tovey, H. (2007) *Playing Outdoors: Spaces and Places, Risk and Challenge*. Maidenhead: Open University Press.

Valentine, G., Holloway, S. and Bingham, N. (2000) 'Transforming cyberspace: Children's interventions in the new public sphere', in S. Holloway and G. Valentine (eds), *Children's Geographies: Playing, Living, Learning*. London: Routledge.

WAG (Welsh Assembly Government) (2008) *Learning and Teaching Pedagogy*. Cardiff: Welsh Assembly Government.

WAG (Welsh Assembly Government) (2009) *The Foundation Phase Outdoor Learning Handbook*. Cardiff: Welsh Assembly Government.

Waite, S. and Pratt, N. (2011) 'Theoretical perspectives on learning outside the classroom: Relationships between learning and place', in S. Waite (ed.), *Children Learning Outside the Classroom*. London: Sage.

Waite, S. (ed.) (2011) *Children Learning Outside the Classroom*. London: Sage.

Waller, S. (2011) 'Adults are essential: The roles of adults outdoors' in J. White (ed.), *Outdoor Provision in the Early Years*. London: Sage.

Waller, T. (2006) 'Don't come too close to my Octopus Tree: Recording and evaluating young children's perspectives on outdoor learning', *Children, Youth and Environment*, 16 (2): 75–104.

Waller, T. (2007) 'The Trampoline and the Swamp Monster with 18 heads: Outdoor play in the Foundation Stage and Foundation Phase', *Education 3–13*, 35 (4): 393–407.

Ward, C. (1990) *The Child in the City*. London: Bedford Square Press.

Waters, J. and Begley, S. (2007) 'Supporting the development of risk-taking behaviour in the early years: An exploratory study', *Education 3–13*, 35 (4): 365–77.

White, J. (2011) *Outdoor Provision in the Early Years*. London: Sage.

Williams-Siegfredson, J. (2005) 'Run the risk', *Nursery World*, 4 (8): 26–7.

Wood, E. and Attfield, J. (2005) *Play, Learning and the Early Childhood Curriculum*, 2nd edn. London: Paul Chapman Publishing.

CONCLUSION

Amanda Thomas and Karen McInnes

In this book we have looked at pedagogy in the Early Years. A key aim of this book has been to link theory and practice across a range of subjects and topics. By combining practical case studies with theoretical underpinnings, each author has endeavoured to provide real-life examples of how teaching in the Early Years needs to be interactive and innovative. A key aim of this book has been to encourage readers to reflect upon their own teaching experiences through key questions and recommended reading. In this concluding chapter we consider and reflect on what might have been learnt from reading this book and we identify overarching themes and key issues that cross between chapters.

As stated in Chapter 1, key features of this book have included fresh perspectives on delivering the curriculum from an academic and a practitioner point of view. Chapters have demonstrated theoretical perspectives and theory in practice linked to the case studies. Another key feature has been the use of case studies from both England and Wales and, where applicable, differences in approaches have been noted and explored. Chapters have also considered home–school links and the importance of transitions from the Early Years into Years 1 and 2. The chapters have also drawn on both Welsh and English Early Years curricula with Chapter 2 providing an overview of all the UK curricula. All UK curricula take a developmental approach to children's learning and development and each one is based on a philosophy of play acknowledging that children should learn through play-based activities. In the EYFS there are overarching principles that all Early Years practitioners should bear in mind: the uniqueness of the child, learning though positive and, we would argue, playful relationships, having an environment that caters for young children's needs and acknowledging that, although the curricula maybe developmental in nature, children develop at different rates. In Wales the FP offers children opportunities to be part of a learning continuum from ages 3 to 7 years. It is a holistic play-based pedagogy with the child at its centre. It is a stage not age framework where children learn at their own pace through a balance of child-led and adult-led activities. As with the EYFS, it considers each child to be unique and to have their needs met through empowering and enabling environments.

The key themes that have emerged as the book has developed have been the real need for experiential learning in the Early Years and the need for children to be given real-world experiences to develop their knowledge and understanding. Throughout, practitioners have shown their enthusiasm and passion for working with our youngest learners through asking children questions and giving them time to answer as well as answering their questions. This is the basis of a social constructivist approach involving collaborative dialogue that enables the co-construction of knowledge. The case studies have exemplified this approach and demonstrated how practitioners firstly respect and then understand the children they work with to ensure that the dialogue between children and adults is meaningful. To achieve this the importance of observation is highlighted and this is linked to understanding how children develop, although as discussed in Chapter 3 this is not always easy. Another common thread running though all the chapters is the importance of a child-centred, playful approach to practice. Again, the case studies often exemplify the playfulness of practitioners and how this enables children to engage in play themselves. This also links to other themes running through the chapters, such as creativity, exploration, problem-solving and curiosity. These are also part of providing an enabling environment that further develops children's confidence, enjoyment and independence.

The second chapter in the book sets the subsequent chapters into context by investigating the similarities and differences between UK Early Years curricula. Throughout the book there have been examples of activities that foster development (Chapter 3), creativity and imagination (Chapters 5 and 8) and those that nurture children's curiosity (Chapters 6, 7 and 9). Consideration of children's right to play and how to embed a playful pedagogy have been discussed (Chapter 4) and the importance of children's well-being has been explored (Chapter 5). Although each chapter has explored a different topic, there are obvious links between chapters. For example, Chapter 4 has argued the importance of a playful pedagogy, and many of the case studies exemplify such a pedagogy. Chapter 5 discusses the criticality of supporting children's well-being and again throughout the case studies presented in each chapter there is evidence of practitioners ensuring that children's well-being is of paramount importance. In the case studies the children are engaged in different activities but each activity is experiential, recognising that for our youngest learners knowledge generation needs to be practical.

Throughout the book academics have worked alongside practitioners and this has allowed the academics to have a fresh perspective on innovative practice that is going on in Early Years settings in England and Wales. This is an example of what Robson (2011) terms real-world research as it endeavours to provide insight into real-life pedagogy provided by practitioners working in different settings. For the practitioners, writing these chapters has allowed them to reflect upon their pedagogy and to reconnect with the theoretical underpinnings that their practice espouses. For the academics, it has allowed them to gain insight into the innovative practices that go on with our youngest learners. Hopefully, for our readers the complexity and theoretical underpinning of Early Years practice have been explained and exemplified through the case studies and subsequent discussion.

Both the EYFP and EYFS state that all children should develop holistically and to their full potential. We would argue that all those working in Early Years education should also develop to their full potential. The innovative approach employed in this book of Early Years academics and practitioners working together and engaging in joint reflection and dialogue that mirror effective Early Years practice, ensures this development in both understanding and practice. It is stated that effective professional development involves collaboration and expert challenge (DfE, 2016), both of which were in evidence as these chapters were written. Further joint learning, continuous professional development and the undertaking of higher degrees ensure that those working in Early Years education develop to their full potential and continue to be lifelong learners, ultimately benefiting the children they work with.

References

DfE (Department for Education) (2016) *Standard for Teachers' Professional Development*. www.gov.uk/government/uploads/system/uploads/attachment_data/file/537030/160712_-_PD_standard.pdf (accessed 17 December 2016).
Robson, C. (2011) *Real World Research*, 3rd edn. Chichester: Wiley–Blackwell.

INDEX